I AM

Empowered
Unleashing Divine Power with Positive Declarations

Gerard Assey

I AM
Empowered
Unleashing Divine Power with Positive Declarations
By
Gerard Assey
© Copyright 2023 by Author

Published by:
Gerard Assey
19/18, Palli Arasan Street
Anna Nagar East
Chennai - 600 102

ISBN: 978-93-92492-92-1

Table of Contents

Acknowledgment and Honor

In the creation of this book, **'I AM Empowered:** *Unleashing Divine Power with Positive Declarations'* there exists an indebtedness of gratitude to an exceptional Man of GOD, whose wisdom and teachings have profoundly impacted not only me, but countless lives around the world.

This work is a manifestation of a revelation received on the 8th of September 2023 during one of the teachings delivered at one of the many schools by our esteemed spiritual father- The Esteemed Prophet Jerome Fernando. It was in that moment, as the words of wisdom flowed, that a divine spark ignited within, compelling me to embark on this book with the intention of sharing life-transforming truths unveiled.

For nearly a decade, this extraordinary Man of GOD has been more than a spiritual father- he has been a mentor, a life coach, and a guiding light. His teachings have consistently propelled individuals from revelation to elevation, infusing their lives with purpose, faith, and power.

I extend my heartfelt gratitude to our spiritual father for his unwavering dedication to the spiritual growth and empowerment of countless souls. His unwavering commitment to the service of God has served as a beacon of inspiration, and his life stands as a testament to the transformative power of faith and positive declarations.

To our revered spiritual father-Prophet Jerome, you are not only a source of inspiration, but you are also a true model of faith and a guiding light on our spiritual journey. Your impact on our lives is immeasurable, and we honor you with the deepest respect and gratitude.

With profound appreciation and deep gratitude

Introduction

In the Gospel of John, chapter 18, verse 5, there is a remarkable moment when Jesus of Nazareth, the Son of God, utters two simple words that carry profound meaning: "I AM." The response to His declaration is astonishing – His adversaries, those who had come to arrest Him, "drew back and fell to the ground." These two words, "I AM," spoken by Jesus, were not ordinary; they were a revelation of the divine power within Him AND Who HE was, is and will be.

In this moment, we witness the significance of the name "I AM." It is a name that encapsulates the very essence of God as revealed to Moses in the book of Exodus. It is a name of power, authority, and divine presence. "I AM" signifies the eternal, self-existent, and unchanging nature of the Almighty. And as believers, we are not only called to acknowledge this name, but we are also invited to embody it in our lives.

The Power of Consciousness: The encounter in John 18 serves as a powerful reminder that divine power does not work until we are conscious of it- it must get into our spirit. It is not merely a matter of having more of the Holy Spirit within us, but it is about becoming more conscious of the God who dwells within us. The moment Jesus said, "I AM He," the very ground upon which His adversaries stood quaked, and they were compelled to take a step back in awe and reverence.

The Conscious Use of "I AM": "I AM" is not just a casual phrase; it is the name of the Lord, the source of all power and existence. As believers, we are created in the image of God, and within us resides the divine power that comes from acknowledging and aligning ourselves with the "I AM." However, power does not work, until we are conscious of it. It is, therefore, of paramount importance that we use "I AM" in a conscious and positive manner.

What have you been confessing and declaring about your own situations and over your life? When you encounter physical discomfort, don't express it in the negative: *"I AM not feeling well..."* Instead, affirm, *"Lord Jesus, I thank You that by Your stripes, I AM healed"* (1 Peter 2:24).

During financial challenges, don't ever say: *"I AM down..."* or *"I AM totally broke..."*, but rather Proclaim, *"The LORD is my shepherd; I AM never in want"* (Psalm 23:1).

We live in a world filled with fear due to terrorism, negativism and diseases. Yet, as believers, we must never speak negative words and succumb to fear. We must speak God's Word and exercise authority over these situations. Like the psalmist, we will declare, *"He is my refuge and my fortress; my God, in Him I will trust."*

Discover what God's Word says about your circumstances, believe it, and declare it. God's Word never returns void (Isaiah 55:11). What you believe and declare in faith, you will see come to pass!

Negative declarations, such as "I AM unwell" or "I AM weak," are a misuse of this divine name. We inadvertently diminish the power within us when we use "I AM" in a negative context. Instead, we should harness the incredible potential of this name by making positive declarations that align with God's Word and our true identity in Christ.

Stirring Up Our Consciousness: This book, '**I AM Empowered:** *Unleashing Divine Power with Positive Declarations'* aims to guide believers on a transformative journey of self-discovery and faith-building. It is designed to help you become more conscious of the "I AM" within you and to unleash its potential in your life. Through a series of 31 decrees and declarations (one for each day of the month) on 30 various topics that you could choose from, this book will empower you to:

- ✓ Cultivate faith and confidence in God's Word.
- ✓ Walk in alignment with your true identity as a child of God.
- ✓ Experience the miraculous power of positive declarations.
- ✓ Transform your thinking and speech to be in harmony with the Word of God.
- ✓ Live a life of purpose, influence, and fulfillment.

As you read and meditate through the pages of this book, may you be inspired and equipped to embrace the power of "I AM" and declare it over your life all through each day, with intention and faith.

Together, let us draw back the veil of ordinary existence and step into the extraordinary realm of God's divine presence and power, manifesting His glory in our everyday lives.

Applying the Power of Positive Declarations in Daily Life

In the chapters to follow, we've explored the incredible potential of positive declarations and the transformative power of the "I AM." We've delved into 30 various aspects of life, from faith and healing to purpose and resilience, providing you with 31 declarations for each topic. Now, it's time to put this wisdom into daily practice and experience a profound shift in your mindset, consciousness, and identity.

Action Plan: Cultivating Daily Positive Declarations

1. Prepare Yourself:
   - ✓ Preferably first thing in the morning, when the mind is fresh.
   - ✓ Find a quiet place, with no disturbances. Use this place every day. Let this be your 'prayer altar'
   - ✓ Close the door
   - ✓ Have a pen and pad
   - ✓ Choose a time when not tired
   - ✓ Must get into the right mood/ mindset: You can't pray if mood is not right- the mind needs to be focused
   - ✓ Right music can help you to get into this mindset
   - ✓ Sit/ breathe with eyes closed
   - ✓ Practice quietness- it calms the flesh
   - ✓ Don't think of anything
   - ✓ Quietness is more powerful than fasting
   - ✓ The spirit takes over- it guides the mind
   - ✓ Mind swirls without you realizing

Now Begin to Focus on the Matter to be Resolved
2. Morning Declarations:
- ✓ Start each day with a declaration of faith and purpose. Choose one or more topics or declarations from the book that resonate with you, your situation or the challenge you are facing, and speak them aloud.
- ✓ Use this time to connect with the presence of God within you and strengthen your consciousness of the "I AM."
- ✓ As you declare these statements, visualize them becoming a reality in your life. See yourself living in alignment with the "I AM" of God.

2. Journaling Your Declarations:
- ✓ Create a "Declaration Journal" to record your chosen declarations for the day. Write down the date and your selected declarations in the morning and evening.
- ✓ Reflect on how these declarations impact your thoughts and emotions throughout the day.

4. Affirmation Cards:
- ✓ Create affirmation cards with your favorite declarations and carry them with you throughout the day. Whenever you have a moment, pull out a card and repeat the declaration. (I am NOT recommending on your phone as it could distract you)
- ✓ These cards serve as visual reminders to stay aligned with the "I AM" and reinforce your faith.

5. Accountability Partner:
- ✓ Share your journey with your life partner, a trusted friend or accountability partner. Encourage each other to embrace the power

of positive declarations and hold one another accountable.
- ✓ Discuss your experiences, challenges, and victories on this transformative path.

6. Weekly Reflection:
- ✓ Dedicate time each week for reflection and review. Assess your progress in applying positive declarations in your daily life.
- ✓ Celebrate your achievements and identify areas where you can deepen your practice.

7. Scripture Study:
- ✓ Dive deeper into the Word of God to fortify your faith and understanding. Study scriptures related to the topics covered in the book.
- ✓ Connect these scriptures with your declarations to enhance their impact and significance.

8. Gratitude and Celebration:
- ✓ Express gratitude for the positive changes you witness in your life as a result of declaring the "I AM." Celebrate even the small victories.
- ✓ Gratitude enhances your receptivity to God's blessings and reinforces a positive mindset.

9. Ongoing Learning:
- ✓ Continue to learn and grow in your understanding of the "I AM" and HIS significance in your life. Explore books, sermons (of my mentor and coach: Prophet Jerome Fernando), and resources (Join the AMP Schools of PJFM Ministries) that deepen your faith.
- ✓ Share your insights with others, spreading the transformative power of positive declarations.

10. Renewing the Mind and Conscience:

✓ Recognize that the renewal of your mind and conscience is an ongoing process. It requires consistent practice and a commitment to aligning your thoughts, words, and actions with the "I AM" of God.
✓ Be patient with yourself, knowing that transformation takes time, and the journey is as valuable as the destination.

By implementing this action plan into your daily life, you will not only renew your mind and conscience but also become more conscious of who you truly are—an heir of the "I AM," empowered to live a life of purpose, influence, and fulfillment. The "I AM" within you is a source of endless strength, wisdom, and love.

Embrace it, declare it, and watch your life be transformed in remarkable ways.

1. Angels Ministering on Your Behalf

May these declarations and scriptures remind you of the **Presence and Ministry of Angels in your Life**, bringing comfort, protection, guidance, and blessings as they fulfill God's purposes on your behalf.

1. *I AM a believer in the presence of angels, and I trust that God's angels surround me. (Psalm 34:7)*
2. *I AM declaring that I have angels encamped around me, protecting me from harm. (Psalm 91:11)*
3. *I AM aware that angels are sent by God to minister to me and aid me in times of need. (Hebrews 1:14)*
4. *I AM declaring that I have guardian angels who watch over me day and night. (Psalm 91:11-12)*
5. *I AM a person of faith, believing that angels are actively working on my behalf. (Matthew 18:10)*
6. *I AM declaring that I have angels assigned to protect me from accidents and calamities. (Psalm 91:11)*
7. *I AM confident that angels are fighting battles on my behalf in the spiritual realm. (Daniel 10:12-13)*
8. *I AM declaring that I have angels guiding my steps and directing my path. (Proverbs 3:6)*
9. *I AM a believer in divine interventions, knowing that angels can bring supernatural help into my life. (Acts 12:7)*

10. *I AM declaring that I have angels who go before me to prepare the way and open doors of opportunity. (Exodus 23:20)*
11. *I AM a person of prayer, and my prayers activate the involvement of angels in my life. (Luke 22:43)*
12. *I AM declaring that I have angels releasing divine messages and revelations to me. (Matthew 2:13)*
13. *I AM a person of humility, recognizing that God's angels are messengers of His grace and mercy. (Psalm 103:20)*
14. *I AM declaring that I have angels ministering to my physical and emotional needs. (Matthew 4:11)*
15. *I AM a believer in God's supernatural provision, knowing that angels can bring resources into my life. (1 Kings 19:5-7)*
16. *I AM declaring that I have angels who bring comfort and peace during times of distress. (Luke 22:43)*
17. *I AM a person of worship, and my worship invites the presence and ministry of angels. (Psalm 148:2-5)*
18. *I AM declaring that I have angels who help me resist temptations and walk in righteousness. (Matthew 4:6)*
19. *I AM a believer in divine appointments, recognizing that angels can orchestrate encounters for my benefit. (Acts 10:3)*
20. *I AM declaring that I have angels who bring healing and restoration to my body and soul. (John 5:4)*

21. I AM a person of gratitude, thanking God for His provision through the ministry of angels. (Psalm 103:21)

22. I AM declaring that I have angels who release supernatural favor and opportunities into my life. (Genesis 24:40)

23. I AM a person of faithfulness, and my faith activates the assistance of angels in my life. (Psalm 91:11)

24. I AM declaring that I have angels who are a part of God's heavenly army, fighting for my victory. (2 Kings 6:16-17)

25. I AM a believer in divine protection, knowing that angels guard me from unseen dangers. (Psalm 34:7)

26. I AM declaring that I have angels who bring wisdom and guidance in my decision-making. (Genesis 24:7)

27. I AM a person of humility, recognizing that I AM not alone but surrounded by a heavenly host. (2 Kings 6:16)

28. I AM declaring that I have angels who are instruments of God's grace and blessing in my life. (Genesis 24:1)

29. I AM a person of discernment, recognizing the supernatural activity of angels in my life. (Luke 2:13-14)

30. I AM declaring that I have angels who join in worship and praise to God with me. (Revelation 5:11-12)

31. I AM confident that angels are active in my life, ministering to me in accordance with God's perfect will. (Hebrews 13:2)

2. Anointing (The Power for Daily Living-The Miraculous Ability-The Unction to Function under Every Situation)

May these declarations and scriptures empower you to live a life filled with the **Anointing of the Holy Spirit, allowing you to function effectively** under every situation and experience God's miraculous ability in all aspects of your life.

1. *I AM anointed by the Holy Spirit, and His anointing empowers me for every situation. (1 John 2:27)*
2. *I AM declaring that I have the anointing to do all things through Christ who strengthens me. (Philippians 4:13)*
3. *I AM a vessel of God's anointing, and His anointing breaks every yoke of bondage. (Isaiah 10:27)*
4. *I AM anointed with fresh oil daily, and God's presence flows through me like a river. (Psalm 92:10)*
5. *I AM declaring that I have the anointing to heal the sick, cast out demons, and proclaim the gospel. (Mark 16:17-18)*
6. *I AM a person of spiritual discernment, and the anointing of the Holy Spirit guides my decisions. (1 Corinthians 2:14)*
7. *I AM anointed to bring good news to the afflicted, bind up the brokenhearted, and proclaim liberty to the captives. (Isaiah 61:1)*

8. I AM declaring that I have the anointing to speak God's Word with boldness and authority. (Acts 4:31)

9. I AM a believer in the anointing of God's wisdom, and His wisdom guides my path. (James 1:5)

10. I AM anointed to be a light in a dark world, shining with the power of God's presence. (Matthew 5:14)

11. I AM declaring that I have the anointing to overcome every obstacle and challenge I face. (1 John 4:4)

12. I AM a person of prayer, and my prayers are anointed by the Holy Spirit's intercession. (Romans 8:26)

13. I AM anointed for divine appointments, and God orchestrates encounters to fulfill His purposes through me. (Proverbs 16:9)

14. I AM declaring that I have the anointing to preach the gospel and make disciples of all nations. (Matthew 28:19-20)

15. I AM anointed with the oil of joy, and God's joy is my strength in every circumstance. (Nehemiah 8:10)

16. I AM a vessel of God's love, and His love flows through me, touching hearts and lives. (1 Corinthians 13:2)

17. I AM anointed for leadership, and I lead with humility and the guidance of the Holy Spirit. (Matthew 20:26-28)

18. I AM declaring that I have the anointing to see signs, wonders, and miracles follow my ministry. (Mark 16:20)

19. I AM anointed to comfort those who mourn and bring beauty out of ashes. (Isaiah 61:2-3)

20. I AM a person of faith, and my faith activates the anointing of God in my life. (Hebrews 11:6)
21. I AM anointed for creativity and innovation, and God's ideas flow through me. (Exodus 31:3)
22. I AM declaring that I have the anointing to walk in love, forgiveness, and reconciliation. (Colossians 3:13)
23. I AM anointed to be a witness for Christ, sharing His love and truth with the world. (Acts 1:8)
24. I AM a person of humility, recognizing that the anointing comes from God's grace, not my own merit. (2 Corinthians 12:9)
25. I AM anointed for breakthrough, and every obstacle in my path is removed by God's power. (2 Samuel 5:20)
26. I AM declaring that I have the anointing to speak life and blessings into every situation. (Proverbs 18:21)
27. I AM anointed for stewardship, and I use my resources and gifts to advance God's kingdom. (1 Peter 4:10)
28. I AM anointed with the oil of gladness, and I carry God's joy wherever I go. (Psalm 45:7)
29. I AM declaring that I have the anointing to walk in victory, for I AM more than a conqueror through Christ. (Romans 8:37)
30. I AM anointed for transformation, and God's power changes me into His image day by day. (2 Corinthians 3:18)
31. I AM a person of worship, and my worship ushers in the manifest presence of God's anointing. (Psalm 22:3)

3. Christ-Esteem and Christ-Confidence

May these declarations and scriptures empower you to cultivate **Christ-confidence and Christ-esteem**, recognizing your worth and identity in Him.

1. *I AM confident in Christ, for in Him, I can do all things. (Philippians 4:13)*
2. *I AM declaring that I AM fearfully and wonderfully made by God. (Psalm 139:14)*
3. *I AM a person of worth, knowing that I AM chosen and loved by Christ. (1 Thessalonians 1:4)*
4. *I AM confident in my identity as a child of God, for I AM adopted into His family. (Ephesians 1:5)*
5. *I AM declaring that I AM a new creation in Christ, and the old has passed away. (2 Corinthians 5:17)*
6. *I AM a person of faith, trusting in Christ's power working in me. (Ephesians 3:20)*
7. *I AM confident in God's promises, knowing that He has plans for my good. (Jeremiah 29:11)*
8. *I AM declaring that I AM deeply loved by God, and His love casts out all fear. (1 John 4:18)*
9. *I AM a person of grace, understanding that I AM saved by God's unmerited favor. (Ephesians 2:8)*
10. *I AM confident in my calling, knowing that God has equipped me for His purposes. (2 Timothy 1:9)*

11. *I AM declaring that I AM an over-comer in Christ, and I have victory over every challenge. (Romans 8:37)*
12. *I AM a person of hope, anchored in the hope that Christ provides. (Hebrews 6:19)*
13. *I AM confident in God's presence with me, for He will never leave nor forsake me. (Deuteronomy 31:6)*
14. *I AM declaring that I AM a temple of the Holy Spirit, and God dwells in me. (1 Corinthians 6:19)*
15. *I AM a person of purpose, recognizing that I AM created for good works in Christ. (Ephesians 2:10)*
16. *I AM confident in my forgiveness through Christ's sacrifice on the cross. (Ephesians 1:7)*
17. *I AM declaring that I AM strong in the Lord and in His mighty power. (Ephesians 6:10)*
18. *I AM a person of peace, experiencing the peace of Christ that surpasses understanding. (Philippians 4:7)*
19. *I AM confident in God's provision, for He supplies all my needs according to His riches. (Philippians 4:19)*
20. *I AM declaring that I AM more than a conqueror through Christ who loves me. (Romans 8:37)*
21. *I AM a person of humility, recognizing that Christ is my example of humility. (Philippians 2:5-8)*
22. *I AM confident in my eternal inheritance in Christ, kept secure by His grace. (1 Peter 1:4-5)*
23. *I AM declaring that I AM a vessel of God's love, sharing His love with others. (1 John 4:7)*

24. I AM a person of wisdom, seeking wisdom from God who gives generously. (James 1:5)
25. I AM confident in God's guidance, trusting that He directs my steps. (Proverbs 3:6)
26. I AM declaring that I AM free in Christ, for where the Spirit of the Lord is, there is freedom. (2 Corinthians 3:17)
27. I AM a person of thanksgiving, offering gratitude for the grace and love of Christ. (Colossians 3:15)
28. I AM confident in God's faithfulness, for He who promised is faithful. (Hebrews 10:23)
29. I AM declaring that I AM an ambassador for Christ, representing His kingdom on earth. (2 Corinthians 5:20)
30. I AM a person of courage, taking bold steps in faith, knowing that God is with me. (Joshua 1:9)
31. I AM confident in Christ's victory over sin and death, and I share in His triumph. (1 Corinthians 15:57)

4. Courage (Living without Fear- A Spirit of a Conqueror)

May these declarations and scriptures empower you to live a life filled with **Courage, Free from Fear, and with the Confidence of a Conqueror in Christ.**

1. *I AM courageous, for the Lord is with me; I will not be afraid. (Psalm 118:6)*
2. *I AM declaring that I AM not given a spirit of fear, but of power, love, and a sound mind. (2 Timothy 1:7)*
3. *I AM an overcomer through Christ, and I have the courage to face any challenge. (Romans 8:37)*
4. *I AM a person of faith, and my faith in God banishes fear from my life. (1 John 4:18)*
5. *I AM declaring that I have courage to be strong and of good courage, knowing that the Lord goes with me. (Deuteronomy 31:6)*
6. *I AM a vessel of God's peace, and His peace guards my heart against fear. (Philippians 4:7)*
7. *I AM a conqueror through Christ, and I can do all things through Him who strengthens me. (Philippians 4:13)*
8. *I AM declaring that I AM bold and courageous, for the Lord is my helper. (Hebrews 13:6)*
9. *I AM a person of wisdom, and I have discernment to overcome fear and make wise decisions. (Proverbs 3:21)*
10. *I AM a believer in God's promises, and His promises give me the courage to face the future without fear. (Joshua 1:9)*

11. *I AM declaring that I have the courage to stand firm in the face of adversity, knowing that God is with me. (Isaiah 41:10)*
12. *I AM a person of hope, and my hope in God dispels fear and anxiety. (Psalm 42:11)*
13. *I AM a child of God, and His perfect love casts out all fear from my heart. (1 John 4:18)*
14. *I AM declaring that I have courage to be strong and courageous, not terrified or discouraged. (Joshua 1:9)*
15. *I AM a person of prayer, and in times of fear, I seek God's presence and guidance through prayer. (Philippians 4:6-7)*
16. *I AM a vessel of faith, and my faith in God's promises gives me the courage to face any giants in my life. (1 Samuel 17:45)*
17. *I AM declaring that I AM not anxious about anything, but with prayer and thanksgiving, I overcome fear. (Philippians 4:6)*
18. *I AM a person of humility, recognizing that God's strength is made perfect in my weakness. (2 Corinthians 12:9)*
19. *I AM a believer in the Lord, and I have the courage to trust in Him with all my heart. (Proverbs 3:5-6)*
20. *I AM declaring that I AM fearless because God has not given me a spirit of fear. (2 Timothy 1:7)*
21. *I AM a person of courage, and I AM strong and courageous in the Lord. (Ephesians 6:10)*
22. *I AM a recipient of God's strength, and His strength empowers me to overcome fear. (Isaiah 40:31)*
23. *I AM declaring that I AM brave and fearless, for God is with me wherever I go. (Joshua 1:9)*

24. *I AM a person of gratitude, and I thank God for His courage that enables me to face challenges head-on. (1 Thessalonians 5:18)*

25. *I AM a conqueror in Christ, and I have the courage to face trials and tribulations with unwavering faith. (Romans 8:37)*

26. *I AM declaring that I AM not dismayed, for the Lord is my God who strengthens me. (Isaiah 41:10)*

27. *I AM a person of endurance, and I endure fear and doubt with a spirit of perseverance. (James 1:3)*

28. *I AM a believer in God's protection, and I find courage in knowing that God is my refuge and strength. (Psalm 46:1)*

29. *I AM declaring that I have the courage to walk in the path of righteousness, trusting in God's guidance. (Psalm 23:3)*

30. *I AM a person of courage, and I declare that I AM more than a conqueror through Him who loved me. (Romans 8:37)*

31. *I AM courageous, and my courage comes from the Lord, who is my strength and fortress. (Psalm 27:1)*

5. Dominion
(Walking in Authority of Who You are in Christ)

May these declarations and scriptures empower you to **Walk Boldly in Your Authority and Dominion as a Believer in Christ**, bringing His kingdom to earth and advancing His purposes.

1. *I AM a child of God, and I have authority over all the power of the enemy. (Luke 10:19)*
2. *I AM declaring that I have been given a spirit of power, love, and a sound mind. (2 Timothy 1:7)*
3. *I AM an overcomer through Christ, and I tread upon serpents and scorpions, and nothing can harm me. (Luke 10:19)*
4. *I AM a conqueror in all things, for I can do all things through Christ who strengthens me. (Philippians 4:13)*
5. *I AM declaring that I have authority to trample on snakes and scorpions and to overcome all the power of the enemy. (Luke 10:19)*
6. *I AM a joint-heir with Christ, and I share in His authority and dominion. (Romans 8:17)*
7. *I AM a person of faith, and my faith activates my authority in Christ. (Mark 11:23)*
8. *I AM declaring that I have authority to bind and loose, and my prayers have power in the spiritual realm. (Matthew 18:18)*
9. *I AM filled with the Holy Spirit, and His power empowers me to walk in authority. (Acts 1:8)*

10. *I AM a person of prayer, and my prayers release God's authority and bring His kingdom to earth. (Matthew 6:10)*
11. *I AM declaring that I have been delivered from the domain of darkness and transferred into the kingdom of God's beloved Son. (Colossians 1:13)*
12. *I AM a vessel of God's authority, and I speak with authority and boldness in Christ. (Acts 4:31)*
13. *I AM a servant of righteousness, yielding my members to God as instruments of righteousness. (Romans 6:13)*
14. *I AM declaring that I have authority to cast out demons and set the captives free. (Mark 16:17)*
15. *I AM a person of discernment, recognizing the schemes of the devil and standing firm against them. (Ephesians 6:11)*
16. *I AM a proclaimer of the gospel, sharing the good news with authority and conviction. (Mark 16:15)*
17. *I AM declaring that I have the authority to lay hands on the sick, and they will recover. (Mark 16:18)*
18. *I AM a citizen of the kingdom of heaven, and I exercise my authority as an ambassador for Christ. (2 Corinthians 5:20)*
19. *I AM a person of love, and I use my authority to bless and serve others. (Galatians 5:13)*
20. *I AM declaring that I have been seated with Christ in heavenly places, far above all principalities and powers. (Ephesians 2:6)*

21. *I AM a person of wisdom, and I use my authority with wisdom and discernment. (James 1:5)*

22. *I AM a believer in the name of Jesus, and I command and decree in His name with authority. (John 14:13)*

23. *I AM declaring that I have authority to speak life and blessings into situations and circumstances. (Proverbs 18:21)*

24. *I AM a child of light, exposing the works of darkness with the authority of truth. (Ephesians 5:11)*

25. *I AM a person of humility, recognizing that my authority comes from God and not my own strength. (James 4:10)*

26. *I AM declaring that I have authority over fear and doubt, and I walk in faith and confidence. (2 Timothy 1:7)*

27. *I AM a defender of the faith, contending earnestly for the authority of God's Word. (Jude 1:3)*

28. *I AM a person of grace, extending God's authority with love and compassion. (Ephesians 4:32)*

29. *I AM declaring that I have authority to bind the works of darkness and release the power of God. (Matthew 16:19)*

30. *I AM a conqueror in Christ, and I exercise my authority to overcome every obstacle. (Romans 8:37)*

31. *I AM a believer in the finished work of the cross, and I walk in the authority of my identity in Christ. (2 Corinthians 5:17)*

6. Family

May these declarations and scriptures on **Family** inspire and strengthen your relationships and your role within your family.

1. *I AM blessed with a loving and harmonious family, for God sets the lonely in families. (Psalm 68:6)*
2. *I AM declaring that my household serves the Lord, and we choose to follow Him faithfully. (Joshua 24:15)*
3. *I AM committed to loving and honoring my family, for love covers a multitude of sins. (1 Peter 4:8)*
4. *I AM a parent who trains up my children in the way they should go, and they will not depart from it. (Proverbs 22:6)*
5. *I AM a spouse who loves and cherishes my partner, as Christ loves the church. (Ephesians 5:25)*
6. *I AM a source of encouragement and support to my family, building them up in love. (1 Thessalonians 5:11)*
7. *I AM declaring that my family's home is a place of peace and God's presence. (Psalm 122:7)*
8. *I AM grateful for my family, for every good and perfect gift is from above. (James 1:17)*
9. *I AM a parent who leads by example, demonstrating the fruits of the Spirit in my life. (Galatians 5:22-23)*
10. *I AM a prayerful parent, committing my family's needs to the Lord and seeking His guidance. (Philippians 4:6-7)*

11. *I AM a parent who imparts wisdom and godly values to my children, shaping their character. (Proverbs 4:10-13)*
12. *I AM declaring that my family is united in faith and purpose, serving the Lord together. (1 Corinthians 1:10)*
13. *I AM a spouse who values and respects my partner, recognizing their unique worth. (Ephesians 5:33)*
14. *I AM a parent who nurtures a spirit of gratitude and contentment in my family. (Philippians 4:11)*
15. *I AM a parent who forgives and extends grace, just as Christ forgives me. (Colossians 3:13)*
16. *I AM declaring that my family's home is a place of joy and laughter. (Proverbs 17:22)*
17. *I AM a parent who teaches my children the fear of the Lord, the beginning of wisdom. (Proverbs 9:10)*
18. *I AM a parent who leads with love, knowing that love is the greatest commandment. (Matthew 22:37-39)*
19. *I AM a parent who listens and understands, fostering open communication in my family. (Proverbs 18:13)*
20. *I AM declaring that my family is a light to the world, shining God's love and grace. (Matthew 5:16)*
21. *I AM a parent who exemplifies patience and kindness, for love is patient and kind. (1 Corinthians 13:4)*
22. *I AM a parent who seeks wisdom and discernment in guiding my family's decisions. (James 1:5)*

23. I AM a parent who trusts in the Lord's provision for my family's needs. *(Philippians 4:19)*

24. I AM declaring that my family is covered by the protection and favor of the Lord. *(Psalm 5:12)*

25. I AM a parent who sets godly boundaries, teaching my family the importance of discipline. *(Proverbs 22:15)*

26. I AM a parent who exemplifies faith and trust in God's plan for my family's future. *(Proverbs 3:5-6)*

27. I AM declaring that my family is filled with grace and forgiveness, reconciling hearts. *(Colossians 3:13)*

28. I AM a parent who leads my family in worship and devotion, putting God first in our lives. *(Matthew 6:33)*

29. I AM a parent who encourages and supports my children's dreams and aspirations. *(Philippians 4:13)*

30. I AM declaring that my family's legacy is one of faith, hope, and love. *(1 Corinthians 13:13)*

31. I AM grateful for the gift of family, for they are a treasure from the Lord. *(Psalm 127:3)*

7. Favor and Grace of GOD

May these declarations and scriptures on **God's Favor and Grace** empower you to live a life filled with His blessings and goodness.

1. *I AM favored by God, for His favor surrounds me as a shield. (Psalm 5:12)*
2. *I AM declaring that I have found favor in God's sight, just as Noah did. (Genesis 6:8)*
3. *I AM a recipient of God's abundant grace, and His grace is sufficient for me. (2 Corinthians 12:9)*
4. *I AM favored and chosen by God, being a part of His royal priesthood and holy nation. (1 Peter 2:9)*
5. *I AM declaring that I have favor with both God and man, just as Jesus did. (Luke 2:52)*
6. *I AM walking in divine favor, for the eyes of the Lord are upon the righteous. (Psalm 34:15)*
7. *I AM a vessel of God's grace, experiencing His unmerited favor in every area of my life. (Ephesians 2:8-9)*
8. *I AM declaring that I AM blessed with the grace of our Lord Jesus Christ, who became poor that I might become rich. (2 Corinthians 8:9)*
9. *I AM a child of God, and His favor rests upon His children, guiding their steps. (Psalm 37:23)*
10. *I AM an heir of God's promises, for all the promises of God find their "Yes" in Christ. (2 Corinthians 1:20)*

11. *I AM declaring that God's favor goes before me, opening doors no one can shut. (Revelation 3:8)*

12. *I AM a grateful recipient of God's grace, and His grace empowers me to live a godly life. (Titus 2:11-12)*

13. *I AM favored and beloved in Christ, redeemed and forgiven through His blood. (Ephesians 1:7-8)*

14. *I AM declaring that I AM clothed with God's favor as with a shield, and His favor adorns my life. (Psalm 5:12)*

15. *I AM a person of humility, for God gives grace to the humble but opposes the proud. (James 4:6)*

16. *I AM a recipient of God's favor, and I have been blessed with every spiritual blessing in Christ. (Ephesians 1:3)*

17. *I AM declaring that God's grace is sufficient for me in every trial and challenge I face. (2 Corinthians 12:9)*

18. *I AM a steward of God's grace, sharing His love and favor with those around me. (1 Peter 4:10)*

19. *I AM favored and chosen, adopted as God's child through the riches of His grace. (Ephesians 1:5-6)*

20. *I AM declaring that I AM surrounded by God's favor like a shield, and it protects and guides my life. (Psalm 5:12)*

21. *I AM a person of faith, and my faith activates God's grace and favor in my life. (Ephesians 2:8)*

22. *I AM a believer in Jesus, and through faith, I have access to God's grace and favor. (Romans 5:2)*

23. *I AM declaring that I AM an instrument of God's grace, extending His love and favor to others. (2 Corinthians 5:20)*

24. *I AM favored and blessed, for the Lord takes pleasure in the prosperity of His servants. (Psalm 35:27)*

25. *I AM a receiver of God's abundant grace, and His grace transforms my life from glory to glory. (2 Corinthians 3:18)*

26. *I AM declaring that God's favor rests upon my life, making a way where there seems to be no way. (Isaiah 43:19)*

27. *I AM a child of God's covenant, and His covenant of favor and grace is established in my life. (Psalm 89:28)*

28. *I AM a grateful recipient of God's grace, and His grace empowers me to live a victorious life. (Romans 6:14)*

29. *I AM favored and loved by God, and nothing can separate me from His love and favor. (Romans 8:38-39)*

30. *I AM declaring that I AM a person of gratitude, recognizing and thanking God for His abundant favor and grace in my life. (Colossians 3:17)*

31. *I AM an ambassador of God's grace and favor, reflecting His goodness to a world in need. (2 Corinthians 5:20)*

8. GOD's Love for You

May these declarations and scriptures remind you of the **Depth and Breadth of GOD's Love for You**, filling your heart with the assurance of His unfailing and unconditional love.

1. *I AM deeply loved by God, for He has loved me with an everlasting love. (Jeremiah 31:3)*
2. *I AM declaring that I AM a beloved child of God, chosen and cherished. (1 John 3:1)*
3. *I AM secure in God's love, knowing that nothing can separate me from His love. (Romans 8:38-39)*
4. *I AM confident in God's faithfulness, and His love endures forever. (Psalm 136:26)*
5. *I AM declaring that I AM accepted and approved by God through His boundless love. (Ephesians 1:6)*
6. *I AM forgiven and cleansed by God's love, for His love covers a multitude of sins. (1 Peter 4:8)*
7. *I AM a recipient of God's perfect love, and His love casts out all fear. (1 John 4:18)*
8. *I AM declaring that I AM the apple of God's eye, and He watches over me with great affection. (Psalm 17:8)*
9. *I AM chosen by God's love, predestined for His purpose and calling. (Romans 8:29)*
10. *I AM deeply valued by God, for I AM fearfully and wonderfully made. (Psalm 139:14)*
11. *I AM declaring that I AM filled with God's love, and His love overflows in my heart. (Romans 5:5)*

12. I AM a person of compassion, reflecting God's love to others. (1 John 4:11)
13. I AM forgiven and reconciled to God through His great love and grace. (Ephesians 2:4-5)
14. I AM declaring that I AM empowered by God's love to love others unconditionally. (1 John 4:7)
15. I AM an heir of God's promises, secured by His covenant love. (Romans 8:17)
16. I AM a person of gratitude, thanking God for His love that never fails. (Psalm 136:26)
17. I AM chosen to bear fruit, abiding in God's love as a branch in the vine. (John 15:9-10)
18. I AM declaring that I AM a living testimony of God's love, reflecting His glory. (2 Corinthians 3:18)
19. I AM a person of hope, anchored in God's love that gives me confidence in the future. (Romans 5:5)
20. I AM a vessel of God's love, sharing His love with others through words and actions. (1 John 3:18)
21. I AM declaring that I AM a recipient of God's mercy and compassion because of His great love. (Lamentations 3:22-23)
22. I AM a person of patience, bearing with others in love as God bears with me. (Ephesians 4:2)
23. I AM transformed by God's love, allowing His love to renew my mind and heart. (Romans 12:2)
24. I AM declaring that I AM free from condemnation, for God's love has set me free. (Romans 8:1-2)

25. I AM a person of faith, believing in the depth and breadth of God's love for me. (Ephesians 3:17-19)

26. I AM a recipient of God's grace, saved by His love and not by my own works. (Ephesians 2:8-9)

27. I AM declaring that I AM strengthened by God's love in times of weakness. (2 Corinthians 12:9)

28. I AM a person of humility, recognizing that God's love is a gift I can never earn. (Romans 5:8)

29. I AM confident in God's love, knowing that His plans for me are for my welfare and not for evil. (Jeremiah 29:11)

30. I AM declaring that I AM filled with the fullness of God's love, able to love others as He loves me. (Ephesians 3:19)

31. I AM eternally grateful for God's love that has redeemed, transformed, and adopted me into His family. (Ephesians 1:5)

9. Gratitude and Thankfulness

May these declarations and scriptures inspire and remind you to cultivate a **Heart of Gratitude and Thankfulness** in all aspects of your life.

1. *I AM a grateful person, and I give thanks to the Lord for His abundant blessings. (Psalm 106:1)*
2. *I AM declaring that I AM thankful in all circumstances, for this is God's will for me. (1 Thessalonians 5:18)*
3. *I AM a person of gratitude, recognizing that every good gift comes from God above. (James 1:17)*
4. *I AM thankful for the simple joys of life, finding contentment in God's provision. (1 Timothy 6:6)*
5. *I AM declaring that I AM a cheerful giver, freely sharing my blessings with others. (2 Corinthians 9:7)*
6. *I AM grateful for God's unfailing love, which endures forever. (Psalm 136:26)*
7. *I AM a person of praise, magnifying the Lord and exalting His name in thanksgiving. (Psalm 69:30)*
8. *I AM thankful for the gift of salvation, knowing that I AM redeemed by the blood of Christ. (Ephesians 1:7)*
9. *I AM declaring that I AM a person of gratitude, counting my blessings and naming them one by one. (Psalm 103:2)*
10. *I AM thankful for the beauty of creation, marveling at God's handiwork in the world around me. (Psalm 19:1)*

11. *I AM a person of humility, acknowledging that every good and perfect gift comes from above. (James 1:17)*

12. *I AM grateful for the people in my life, cherishing the relationships that bring joy and support. (Proverbs 17:17)*

13. *I AM declaring that I AM a person of gratitude, offering thanks to God for His daily provisions. (Matthew 6:11)*

14. *I AM thankful for the Word of God, which guides me and fills my heart with wisdom. (Psalm 119:105)*

15. *I AM a person of generosity, sharing my blessings with a thankful heart. (2 Corinthians 9:11)*

16. *I AM grateful for God's mercy and forgiveness, knowing that His love covers my sins. (Psalm 103:12)*

17. *I AM declaring that I AM a person of gratitude, rejoicing in the Lord always. (Philippians 4:4)*

18. *I AM thankful for the gift of faith, which strengthens me and brings hope. (Hebrews 11:1)*

19. *I AM a person of kindness, expressing my gratitude through acts of love and compassion. (Colossians 3:12)*

20. *I AM grateful for the peace of God that surpasses all understanding. (Philippians 4:7)*

21. *I AM declaring that I AM a person of gratitude, choosing to focus on the positive and uplifting in life. (Philippians 4:8)*

22. *I AM thankful for the presence of the Holy Spirit, who comforts and guides me. (John 14:26)*

23. I AM a person of hope, believing that God's plans for me are good and filled with hope. (Jeremiah 29:11)
24. I AM grateful for the gift of life, recognizing that each day is a precious blessing. (Psalm 118:24)
25. I AM declaring that I AM a person of gratitude, offering my thanks to God with a joyful heart. (Psalm 9:1)
26. I AM thankful for the strength that God provides, enabling me to overcome challenges. (Philippians 4:13)
27. I AM a person of patience, waiting on the Lord with thanksgiving in my heart. (Psalm 40:1)
28. I AM grateful for the promise of eternal life, knowing that I have a future filled with hope. (1 Peter 1:3)
29. I AM declaring that I AM a person of gratitude, giving thanks to God for His steadfast love. (Psalm 136:1)
30. I AM thankful for the gift of salvation through Jesus Christ, my Savior and Redeemer. (Ephesians 2:8)
31. I AM a person of gratitude, and I will continually praise the Lord for His goodness and faithfulness. (Psalm 145:2)

10. Healing and Wholeness of Health

May these declarations and scriptures on **Healing and Wholeness of Health** bring strength, faith, and encouragement to your life.

1. *I AM a recipient of God's healing power, for He is the Lord who heals all my diseases. (Psalm 103:3)*
2. *I AM free from sickness and infirmity, for by His wounds, I AM healed. (Isaiah 53:5)*
3. *I AM walking in divine health, and no sickness shall prevail against me. (3 John 1:2)*
4. *I AM declaring God's Word over my body, and it brings life and health to my flesh. (Proverbs 4:22)*
5. *I AM a temple of the Holy Spirit, and His presence brings healing to every part of me. (1 Corinthians 6:19)*
6. *I AM releasing forgiveness and love, for a cheerful heart is good medicine. (Proverbs 17:22)*
7. *I AM casting my anxieties on the Lord, knowing that His peace guards my heart and mind. (Philippians 4:6-7)*
8. *I AM renewing my mind daily with the truth, and it transforms my health and well-being. (Romans 12:2)*
9. *I AM trusting in the Lord with all my heart, and He directs my paths to health and wholeness. (Proverbs 3:5-6)*
10. *I AM speaking life-affirming words, for the power of life and death is in the tongue. (Proverbs 18:21)*

11. *I AM a worshiper, and in the presence of God, there is fullness of joy, which strengthens my body. (Psalm 16:11)*

12. *I AM walking in love, which is the greatest healer of all. (1 Corinthians 13:13)*

13. *I AM laying hands on the sick, and they are recovering, for I walk in the authority of Christ. (Mark 16:18)*

14. *I AM seeking wisdom in my health choices, knowing that it is a tree of life. (Proverbs 3:18)*

15. *I AM claiming the promises of God for my health, for they are "Yes" and "Amen" in Christ. (2 Corinthians 1:20)*

16. *I AM a grateful heart, and a merry heart does good like medicine. (Proverbs 17:22)*

17. *I AM abiding in Christ, and His life flows through me, bringing healing to every area of my body. (John 15:4)*

18. *I AM declaring that no weapon formed against me shall prosper, and this includes sickness. (Isaiah 54:17)*

19. *I AM sowing seeds of kindness and reaping a harvest of health and well-being. (Galatians 6:7)*

20. *I AM walking in divine protection, and no evil shall befall me, for the Lord is my refuge. (Psalm 91:9-10)*

21. *I AM believing in the power of prayer, and the fervent prayer of a righteous person avails much. (James 5:16)*

22. *I AM rejoicing in hope, for hope brings strength to my body and soul. (Romans 12:12)*

23. *I AM receiving the peace of Christ, which surpasses all understanding, guarding my heart and mind. (Philippians 4:7)*

24. I AM a steward of my body, honoring God with my choices for health and well-being. (1 Corinthians 6:20)

25. I AM seeking God's guidance in all my health decisions, trusting in His wisdom and discernment. (James 1:5)

26. I AM a conqueror through Christ, and I overcome any health challenge with faith and perseverance. (Romans 8:37)

27. I AM walking in the light of God's Word, and His Word is health and healing to my body. (Proverbs 4:22)

28. I AM releasing stress and anxiety, knowing that a calm and undisturbed mind brings health. (Proverbs 14:30)

29. I AM a vessel of God's healing grace, and I bring His touch of wholeness to those in need. (Matthew 10:8)

30. I AM declaring that I AM fearfully and wonderfully made, and my body is a testament to God's craftsmanship. (Psalm 139:14)

31. I AM thankful for the gift of life and health, and I praise God for His faithfulness in sustaining me. (Psalm 100:4)

11. Healthy Living and Wellness

These declarations affirm your commitment to a **Healthy and Well-balanced Life**, acknowledging God's role in your physical and mental well-being.

1. *I AM committed to maintaining a healthy lifestyle for the glory of God. (1 Corinthians 6:19-20)*
2. *I AM disciplined in regular exercise, honoring my body as God's temple. (1 Timothy 4:8)*
3. *I AM strong and resilient, physically and mentally. (Philippians 4:13)*
4. *I AM filled with God's wisdom to make nutritious food choices. (1 Corinthians 10:31)*
5. *I AM free from unhealthy cravings, as God satisfies my every need. (Philippians 4:19)*
6. *I AM a good steward of my body, prioritizing self-care and rest. (Matthew 11:28-30)*
7. *I AM full of energy and vitality, a testament to God's goodness. (Isaiah 40:31)*
8. *I AM free from the bondage of unhealthy habits, embracing God's freedom. (Galatians 5:1)*
9. *I AM renewed in mind and spirit, casting away anxiety and stress. (Romans 12:2)*
10. *I AM a source of encouragement to others in their wellness journey. (1 Thessalonians 5:11)*
11. *I AM a peace-filled individual, trusting God with my mental well-being. (Philippians 4:6-7)*
12. *I AM mindful of the words I speak over my health and body. (Proverbs 18:21)*
13. *I AM a seeker of balance, aligning my life with God's principles of health. (1 Corinthians 6:12)*

14. I AM free from guilt and condemnation regarding my health choices. *(Romans 8:1)*

15. I AM a receiver of God's healing grace, restoring me when I am unwell. *(James 5:15)*

16. I AM a promoter of joy and laughter, knowing it's good medicine. *(Proverbs 17:22)*

17. I AM filled with God's love, which casts out all fear. *(1 John 4:18)*

18. I AM a carrier of God's peace, which guards my heart and mind. *(Philippians 4:7)*

19. I AM free from comparison, appreciating the unique path of my wellness journey. *(Galatians 6:4)*

20. I AM an over-comer, breaking free from any addiction or bondage. *(2 Corinthians 5:17)*

21. I AM focused on the present moment, releasing worries about the future. *(Matthew 6:34)*

22. I AM a seeker of God's wisdom in all matters of health and well-being. *(James 1:5)*

23. I AM filled with gratitude for the gift of life and health. *(Psalm 107:1)*

24. I AM a contributor to my community's well-being, sharing God's love. *(Matthew 5:13-16)*

25. I AM resilient in the face of challenges, knowing God's grace is sufficient. *(2 Corinthians 12:9)*

26. I AM a believer in God's healing power, trusting Him in sickness and health. *(Psalm 103:3)*

27. I AM a restorer of hope to those struggling with their health. *(Psalm 42:11)*

28. I AM a wise steward of my time, dedicating it to my well-being. *(Ephesians 5:15-16)*

29. I AM empowered by God to make positive changes in my life. (Philippians 2:13)
30. I AM a receiver of God's peace that transcends all understanding. (Philippians 4:7)
31. I AM whole and well in body, mind, and spirit, reflecting God's divine design. (3 John 1:2)

12. Knowing Your Destiny
(Having a Vision)

May these declarations and scriptures inspire and empower you to pursue your **God-given Destiny** with faith, vision, and purpose.

1. *I AM a person of purpose, and I know that God has a plan and destiny for my life. (Jeremiah 29:11)*
2. *I AM declaring that I have a vision for my life, and I write it down, making it plain. (Habakkuk 2:2)*
3. *I AM a believer in God's guidance, and I trust in Him to direct my steps toward my destiny. (Proverbs 3:5-6)*
4. *I AM a seeker of wisdom, and I ask God for wisdom to understand His purpose and vision for my life. (James 1:5)*
5. *I AM declaring that I AM a person of faith, and I walk by faith, not by sight, toward my destiny. (2 Corinthians 5:7)*
6. *I AM a steward of my gifts and talents, using them to fulfill my God-given purpose and vision. (1 Peter 4:10)*
7. *I AM a person of perseverance, and I press on toward the goal for the prize of the upward call of God in Christ Jesus. (Philippians 3:14)*
8. *I AM declaring that I have a vision that makes my heart glad, for a dream fulfilled is a tree of life. (Proverbs 13:12)*
9. *I AM a person of action, taking steps each day to align myself with God's vision for my life. (James 2:17)*

10. *I AM a believer in divine appointments, recognizing that God orders my steps to fulfill His purpose. (Proverbs 16:9)*
11. *I AM declaring that I AM a vessel of God's glory, and I reflect His glory through my destiny. (Isaiah 60:1)*
12. *I AM a person of prayer, seeking God's guidance and revelation for my destiny. (Psalm 25:4)*
13. *I AM a person of courage, and I AM not afraid to step out in faith to pursue my destiny. (Joshua 1:9)*
14. *I AM declaring that I have a vision that propels me forward, for where there is no vision, the people perish. (Proverbs 29:18)*
15. *I AM a believer in divine timing, and I trust that God's timing for my destiny is perfect. (Ecclesiastes 3:1)*
16. *I AM a person of focus, keeping my eyes fixed on Jesus, the author, and finisher of my faith and destiny. (Hebrews 12:2)*
17. *I AM a steward of my resources, using them to support and fulfill my God-given vision. (Luke 16:10)*
18. *I AM declaring that I have a vision that ignites my passion, for passion fuels perseverance. (Romans 12:11)*
19. *I AM a person of character, and I cultivate godly character as I pursue my destiny. (Galatians 5:22-23)*
20. *I AM a believer in divine connections, recognizing that God brings people into my life to help fulfill my destiny. (Proverbs 27:17)*
21. *I AM declaring that I have a vision that is aligned with God's Word, for His Word is a*

lamp to my feet and a light to my path. (Psalm 119:105)

22. *I AM a person of humility, recognizing that my destiny is a gift from God's grace. (Ephesians 2:8-9)*
23. *I AM a person of gratitude, thanking God for His guidance and revelation regarding my destiny. (1 Thessalonians 5:18)*
24. *I AM declaring that I have a vision that inspires others, for my destiny impacts those around me. (Matthew 5:16)*
25. *I AM a believer in perseverance, for I know that I will reap a harvest if I do not give up in pursuing my destiny. (Galatians 6:9)*
26. *I AM a person of hope, trusting that God's plans for my destiny are for my welfare and not for evil. (Jeremiah 29:11)*
27. *I AM declaring that I have a vision that aligns with God's kingdom purposes, for His kingdom is advancing through my destiny. (Matthew 6:33)*
28. *I AM a person of obedience, following God's guidance as I walk toward my destiny. (Deuteronomy 28:1)*
29. *I AM a person of faithfulness, knowing that God is faithful to fulfill His promises regarding my destiny. (Hebrews 10:23)*
30. *I AM declaring that I have a vision that brings glory to God, for my destiny reflects His greatness. (1 Corinthians 10:31)*
31. *I AM a person of destiny, and I trust that God is with me every step of the way as I fulfill His purpose and vision for my life. (Isaiah 41:10)*

13. Leadership and Influence

May these declarations and scriptures inspire and empower you as a **Leader to Positively Influence and Impact** the lives of those you lead.

1. *I AM a leader of integrity, walking in the light as He is in the light. (1 John 1:7)*
2. *I AM declaring that I AM a servant-leader, following the example of Jesus. (Mark 10:45)*
3. *I AM a person of vision, seeking God's guidance in all my leadership endeavors. (Proverbs 29:18)*
4. *I AM a leader of wisdom, seeking wisdom from God who gives generously. (James 1:5)*
5. *I AM declaring that I AM a person of influence, shining as a light in the world. (Matthew 5:14)*
6. *I AM a leader of humility, esteeming others higher than myself. (Philippians 2:3)*
7. *I AM a person of courage, not being afraid or discouraged, for the Lord is with me. (Joshua 1:9)*
8. *I AM declaring that I AM a person of compassion, leading with a heart of love and empathy. (Colossians 3:12)*
9. *I AM a leader of perseverance, not growing weary in doing good. (Galatians 6:9)*
10. *I AM a person of prayer, seeking God's guidance and wisdom in my leadership role. (James 1:5)*
11. *I AM declaring that I AM a person of accountability, leading with transparency and honesty. (Proverbs 11:3)*
12. *I AM a leader of faith, trusting in the Lord with all my heart. (Proverbs 3:5-6)*

13. I AM a person of purpose, knowing that God has called me to influence for His kingdom. (Esther 4:14)

14. I AM declaring that I AM a person of excellence, giving my best in all that I do. (Colossians 3:23)

15. I AM a leader of compassion, showing kindness to those under my influence. (Ephesians 4:32)

16. I AM a person of unity, seeking to bring harmony and agreement among those I lead. (Psalm 133:1)

17. I AM declaring that I AM a person of empowerment, lifting others up and helping them reach their potential. (Proverbs 11:25)

18. I AM a leader of gratitude, acknowledging and appreciating the contributions of others. (1 Thessalonians 5:18)

19. I AM a person of resilience, not giving up in the face of challenges and obstacles. (1 Corinthians 15:58)

20. I AM declaring that I AM a person of courage, standing firm in my convictions and values. (1 Corinthians 16:13)

21. I AM a leader of growth, continuously learning and developing my leadership skills. (Proverbs 2:6)

22. I AM a person of empowerment, equipping and empowering others to lead effectively. (2 Timothy 2:2)

23. I AM declaring that I AM a person of humility, recognizing that leadership is a privilege and responsibility. (1 Peter 5:5)

24. I AM a leader of discernment, seeking God's guidance in making wise decisions. (James 1:5)
25. I AM a person of impact, using my influence to make a positive difference in the lives of others. (Matthew 5:16)
26. I AM declaring that I AM a person of servant-leadership, putting the needs of others before my own. (Mark 10:43-44)
27. I AM a leader of perseverance, enduring through challenges with grace and determination. (Romans 5:3-4)
28. I AM a person of inspiration, motivating and encouraging those I lead. (1 Thessalonians 5:11)
29. I AM declaring that I AM a person of faith, believing that God equips me for every leadership role. (2 Timothy 3:17)
30. I AM a leader of vision, casting a clear and compelling vision for the future. (Proverbs 29:18)
31. I AM a person of humility, recognizing that true leadership is serving and glorifying God. (Matthew 23:11-12)

14. Living a Victorious Life/ Success in Life

These declarations are designed to empower and encourage individuals to **walk in Victory and Success,** relying on their faith in Christ.

1. *I AM Victorious in Christ (1 Corinthians 15:57)*
2. *I AM More than a Conqueror (Romans 8:37)*
3. *I AM Destined for Success (Jeremiah 29:11)*
4. *I AM a Child of the Most High God (Romans 8:16)*
5. *I AM Fearfully and Wonderfully Made for Success (Psalm 139:14)*
6. *I AM Empowered by God's Spirit (Acts 1:8)*
7. *I AM Bold and Confident (Proverbs 28:1)*
8. *I AM Overflowing with God's Blessings (Malachi 3:10)*
9. *I AM Prosperous in All My Ways (Psalm 1:3)*
10. *I AM the Head and not the Tail (Deuteronomy 28:13)*
11. *I AM Walking in God's Favor (Psalm 5:12)*
12. *I AM anointed for Success (Isaiah 10:27)*
13. *I AM a Wise Decision-Maker (James 1:5)*
14. *I AM Living a Life of Abundance (John 10:10)*
15. *I AM Unstoppable in Christ (Philippians 4:13)*
16. *I AM Surrounded by God's Goodness (Psalm 23:6)*
17. *I AM a Success Magnet (Joshua 1:8)*
18. *I AM Walking in Divine Wisdom (Proverbs 2:6)*
19. *I AM Achieving My Goals (Philippians 3:14)*
20. *I AM Focused on God's Plans for Me (Jeremiah 29:11)*
21. *I AM Breaking through Every Barrier (2 Samuel 22:30)*

22. *I AM Living in Abundant Joy (John 15:11)*
23. *I AM a Blessing to Others (Genesis 12:2)*
24. *I AM Receiving Supernatural Favor (Psalm 84:11)*
25. *I AM Claiming God's Promises for Success (2 Corinthians 1:20)*
26. *I AM Confident in My Abilities through Christ (Philippians 4:13)*
27. *I AM Seizing Every Opportunity for Success (Ephesians 5:16)*
28. *I AM Thriving in Adversity (Romans 8:28)*
29. *I AM Living a Purpose-Driven Life (Proverbs 19:21)*
30. *I AM an Ambassador for Christ, Representing His Victory (2 Corinthians 5:20)*
31. *I AM Living a Victorious Life through Faith (1 John 5:4)*

15. On Fire for GOD

May these declarations and scriptures inspire and empower you to **Stay on Fire for GOD**, keeping the flame of the Spirit burning brightly in your life.

1. *I AM on fire for God, and my heart burns with passion for His presence. (Luke 24:32)*
2. *I AM declaring that I AM filled with the Holy Spirit, and His fire consumes every area of my life. (Acts 2:3-4)*
3. *I AM a vessel of God's fire, shining His light in a dark world. (Matthew 5:14)*
4. *I AM a fervent worshiper, worshiping God in spirit and truth. (John 4:24)*
5. *I AM declaring that I AM zealous for good works, serving God with a burning heart. (Titus 2:14)*
6. *I AM a person of prayer, maintaining a constant and fervent prayer life. (1 Thessalonians 5:17)*
7. *I AM a seeker of God's face, desiring His presence above all else. (Psalm 27:8)*
8. *I AM declaring that I AM steadfast and immovable in my faith, always abounding in the work of the Lord. (1 Corinthians 15:58)*
9. *I AM a torchbearer for Christ, carrying His light into every corner of my life. (2 Corinthians 4:6)*
10. *I AM a person of revival, believing that God can ignite revival in my heart and in my community. (2 Chronicles 7:14)*
11. *I AM declaring that I AM a doer of the Word, not just a hearer, keeping the fire of obedience burning. (James 1:22)*

12. *I AM an encourager, lifting up fellow believers and fanning the flames of their faith. (Hebrews 10:24-25)*

13. *I AM a person of holiness, pursuing holiness and allowing the refining fire of God to purify my heart. (1 Peter 1:15-16)*

14. *I AM declaring that I AM a witness for Christ, sharing His gospel with boldness and passion. (Acts 1:8)*

15. *I AM a person of spiritual hunger, continually seeking after God's presence and His Word. (Matthew 5:6)*

16. *I AM a disciple of Jesus, learning from Him and following His example of fervent love and service. (John 13:15)*

17. *I AM declaring that I AM not ashamed of the gospel, for it is the power of God for salvation. (Romans 1:16)*

18. *I AM a person of compassion, demonstrating God's love to others with a burning heart. (Colossians 3:12)*

19. *I AM a steward of God's gifts, using them to build His kingdom and keep the fire of His purpose alive. (1 Peter 4:10)*

20. *I AM declaring that I AM a conqueror through Christ, and His victory fuels my passion for His mission. (Romans 8:37)*

21. *I AM a person of spiritual warfare, wielding the weapons of prayer and God's Word to keep the fire burning brightly. (Ephesians 6:12)*

22. *I AM a disciple-maker, pouring into others and igniting their passion for Christ. (2 Timothy 2:2)*

23. *I AM declaring that I AM filled with joy in the Holy Spirit, and His joy sustains my fervor. (Romans 14:17)*
24. *I AM a person of gratitude, thanking God daily for His presence and grace that keep the fire burning. (1 Thessalonians 5:18)*
25. *I AM a seeker of God's wisdom, knowing that His wisdom keeps the fire of discernment burning brightly. (Proverbs 2:6)*
26. *I AM declaring that I AM a living sacrifice, wholly devoted to God, and my sacrifice keeps the fire ablaze. (Romans 12:1)*
27. *I AM a person of perseverance, enduring through trials and challenges with unwavering faith. (James 1:3-4)*
28. *I AM a giver, sharing my resources and talents to advance God's kingdom and keep the fire of generosity burning. (2 Corinthians 9:7)*
29. *I AM declaring that I AM anointed by the Holy Spirit, and His anointing keeps the fire of God's presence burning within me. (1 John 2:27)*
30. *I AM a person of humility, recognizing that God's grace fuels my passion and keeps me dependent on Him. (James 4:6)*
31. *I AM a vessel of revival, believing that God's fire can spread through my life and ignite the hearts of others. (Acts 3:19)*

16. Patience and Resilience

May these declarations and scriptures inspire and empower you to cultivate **Patience and Resilience** in all areas of your life, trusting in God's strength and enduring through every season.

1. *I AM patient and resilient, trusting in the Lord's timing for my life. (Psalm 27:14)*
2. *I AM declaring that I AM steadfast in my faith, enduring trials with joy. (James 1:2-3)*
3. *I AM a person of perseverance, pressing on toward the goal despite challenges. (Philippians 3:14)*
4. *I AM patient in affliction, knowing that God's grace sustains me. (Romans 12:12)*
5. *I AM declaring that I AM a person of hope, anchored in the promises of God. (Hebrews 6:19)*
6. *I AM resilient in the face of adversity, for Christ's strength empowers me. (2 Corinthians 12:9-10)*
7. *I AM a person of peace, resting in God's presence even in turbulent times. (John 14:27)*
8. *I AM patient in waiting on the Lord, for His plans are perfect and timely. (Isaiah 40:31)*
9. *I AM declaring that I AM an over-comer, conquering challenges through Christ. (Romans 8:37)*
10. *I AM steadfast in my faith, for my hope is in the Lord who does not disappoint. (Romans 5:5)*
11. *I AM patient in adversity, knowing that God works all things for my good. (Romans 8:28)*

12. I AM a person of resilience, bouncing back stronger from setbacks. (Proverbs 24:16)
13. I AM declaring that I AM a person of courage, facing trials with boldness. (Joshua 1:9)
14. I AM patient in my pursuit of righteousness, seeking God's kingdom above all else. (Matthew 6:33)
15. I AM confident in God's faithfulness, knowing that He never leaves nor forsakes me. (Deuteronomy 31:6)
16. I AM resilient in my determination to finish the race set before me. (2 Timothy 4:7)
17. I AM declaring that I AM a person of humility, relying on God's strength in my weakness. (2 Corinthians 12:10)
18. I AM patient in my interactions with others, bearing with one another in love. (Ephesians 4:2)
19. I AM a person of resilience, for the joy of the Lord is my strength. (Nehemiah 8:10)
20. I AM steadfast in my trust in God, knowing that He is my refuge and strength. (Psalm 46:1)
21. I AM patient in waiting on God's guidance, for His ways are higher than my own. (Isaiah 55:9)
22. I AM declaring that I AM a person of peace, guarding my heart and mind in Christ. (Philippians 4:7)
23. I AM resilient in my commitment to God's Word, meditating on it day and night. (Psalm 1:2)
24. I AM patient in seeking wisdom, knowing that it is a treasure from the Lord. (Proverbs 2:6)

25. *I AM a person of hope, for I know that God has a future and a hope for me. (Jeremiah 29:11)*

26. *I AM steadfast in my faith, standing firm on the promises of God. (1 Corinthians 16:13)*

27. *I AM patient in my journey of sanctification, allowing God's work to be completed in me. (Philippians 1:6)*

28. *I AM declaring that I AM a person of gratitude, thanking God for His strength in my weakness. (2 Corinthians 12:9)*

29. *I AM resilient in my love for others, bearing all things, believing all things, and enduring all things. (1 Corinthians 13:7)*

30. *I AM patient in my waiting on the Lord, renewing my strength like eagles. (Isaiah 40:31)*

31. *I AM a person of resilience, knowing that in Christ, I AM more than a conqueror. (Romans 8:37)*

17. Peace and Joy

May these declarations and scriptures on **Peace and Joy** bring comfort, strength, and a sense of God's presence in your life.

1. *I AM a recipient of God's peace, for His peace surpasses all understanding and guards my heart and mind. (Philippians 4:7)*
2. *I AM declaring that I have the peace of Christ, and I let not my heart be troubled. (John 14:27)*
3. *I AM a peacemaker, for I AM blessed as a child of God and called to bring peace to those around me. (Matthew 5:9)*
4. *I AM a person of hope, and the God of hope fills me with joy and peace as I trust in Him. (Romans 15:13)*
5. *I AM a vessel of joy, for the joy of the Lord is my strength, and it overflows from my heart. (Nehemiah 8:10)*
6. *I AM declaring that the joy of the Lord is my strength, and it sustains me in every circumstance. (Nehemiah 8:10)*
7. *I AM an ambassador of peace, bringing the message of reconciliation to a world in need. (2 Corinthians 5:18-19)*
8. *I AM a person of gratitude, giving thanks in all circumstances, for this is God's will for me. (1 Thessalonians 5:18)*
9. *I AM a bearer of good news, and my feet are beautiful because they bring the message of peace. (Isaiah 52:7)*

10. *I AM declaring that I AM surrounded by the peace of God, which transcends all understanding. (Philippians 4:7)*
11. *I AM a joyful worshiper, entering God's presence with thanksgiving and praise. (Psalm 100:4)*
12. *I AM a person of contentment, knowing that godliness with contentment is great gain. (1 Timothy 6:6)*
13. *I AM a believer in the Prince of Peace, and His peace rules in my heart. (Colossians 3:15)*
14. *I AM declaring that I AM filled with the joy of the Holy Spirit, even in trials and tribulations. (Romans 14:17)*
15. *I AM a person of patience, for the fruit of the Spirit includes patience, leading to peace and joy. (Galatians 5:22-23)*
16. *I AM a seeker of God's kingdom, and His righteousness brings joy and peace to my life. (Matthew 6:33)*
17. *I AM a receiver of God's peace, for He promises to keep me in perfect peace when my mind is fixed on Him. (Isaiah 26:3)*
18. *I AM declaring that I AM anxious for nothing, but in everything, I present my requests to God with thanksgiving, experiencing His peace. (Philippians 4:6-7)*
19. *I AM a lover of God's Word, and meditating on it day and night brings delight and peace to my soul. (Psalm 1:2-3)*
20. *I AM a person of forgiveness, extending grace and forgiveness to others as Christ forgave me. (Colossians 3:13)*

21. I AM declaring that the joy of the Lord is my strength, enabling me to overcome every obstacle. (Nehemiah 8:10)

22. I AM a child of God, and His Spirit within me bears the fruit of love, joy, and peace. (Galatians 5:22)

23. I AM a person of faith, and my faith produces peace and joy even in the midst of trials. (Romans 15:13)

24. I AM a person of unity, seeking to live in harmony with others and promoting peace. (Romans 12:18)

25. I AM declaring that I have a peace that transcends understanding, guarding my heart and mind in Christ. (Philippians 4:7)

26. I AM a person of hope, for hope does not disappoint, and it fills my heart with joy and peace. (Romans 5:5)

27. I AM a worshiper of God, and His presence brings fullness of joy and pleasures forevermore. (Psalm 16:11)

28. I AM a child of God's covenant, and His covenant of peace is established in my life. (Isaiah 54:10)

29. I AM declaring that I AM a person of rest, entering God's rest and finding peace for my soul. (Matthew 11:28-30)

30. I AM a believer in the God of peace, and He crushes Satan under my feet, giving me victory. (Romans 16:20)

31. I AM a person of love, joy, and peace, bearing the fruit of the Spirit and reflecting Christ's character. (Galatians 5:22-23)

18. Personal Growth and Development (in Various Areas of Life)

These declarations affirm your commitment to **Personal Growth and Development** in various areas of life, encouraging you to embrace your potential and become the best version of yourself.

1. *I AM continually growing and developing in all areas of my life. (2 Peter 3:18)*
2. *I AM open to learning and improving myself daily. (Proverbs 18:15)*
3. *I AM a lifelong learner, gaining wisdom from every experience. (Proverbs 1:5)*
4. *I AM committed to my personal and professional growth. (Philippians 3:13-14)*
5. *I AM resilient and capable of overcoming any challenge. (Philippians 4:13)*
6. *I AM confident in my abilities and gifts. (2 Timothy 1:7)*
7. *I AM an effective communicator, fostering positive relationships. (Proverbs 18:21)*
8. *I AM disciplined in my habits and pursuits. (1 Corinthians 9:27)*
9. *I AM a goal-setter and achiever, reaching new heights. (Philippians 4:13)*
10. *I AM creative and innovative, finding solutions to complex problems. (Genesis 1:27)*
11. *I AM a source of inspiration and encouragement to others. (Hebrews 10:24)*
12. *I AM organized and manage my time wisely. (Ephesians 5:15-16)*

13. *I AM adaptable and embrace change with grace. (Isaiah 43:19)*
14. *I AM a leader who empowers and uplifts those around me. (Matthew 20:26-28)*
15. *I AM a steward of my resources, using them wisely for growth. (Luke 16:10)*
16. *I AM a person of integrity, living by strong moral principles. (Proverbs 10:9)*
17. *I AM a problem solver, finding opportunities in challenges. (Romans 8:28)*
18. *I AM a visionary, setting my sights on a bright future. (Jeremiah 29:11)*
19. *I AM patient in my journey of growth, knowing it's a lifelong process. (James 1:4)*
20. *I AM self-aware and continually seek self-improvement. (Psalm 139:23-24)*
21. *I AM a positive thinker, focusing on the good in every situation. (Philippians 4:8)*
22. *I AM courageous and step out of my comfort zone to grow. (Joshua 1:9)*
23. *I AM a servant-hearted leader, putting others first. (Mark 10:45)*
24. *I AM a lifelong reader, gaining knowledge from books and wisdom from God's Word. (Proverbs 2:6)*
25. *I AM a mentor and guide for those on their path of growth. (Proverbs 27:17)*
26. *I AM an overcomer, rising above setbacks and obstacles. (Romans 8:37)*
27. *I AM continually renewing my mind and transforming my life. (Romans 12:2)*
28. *I AM a person of excellence, striving for the best in all I do. (Colossians 3:23)*

29. I AM a source of inspiration and empowerment to my community. (Matthew 5:14)
30. I AM wise in my decisions, seeking counsel and guidance from God. (Proverbs 3:5-6)
31. I AM a lifelong seeker of wisdom and understanding. (Proverbs 4:7)

19. Problem Solver-Solution to the World

These declarations affirm your role as a **Problem Solver and a Source of Positive Change in the World**, drawing upon the wisdom and strength found in God's Word.

1. *I AM anointed to bring solutions to the world's challenges, just as Joseph did in Egypt. (Genesis 41:38-40)*
2. *I AM empowered to think creatively and solve complex problems with wisdom from above. (James 1:5)*
3. *I AM a vessel of God's wisdom, and I bring innovative solutions to every situation. (Proverbs 3:5-6)*
4. *I AM a problem solver, and my ideas have the potential to change lives and impact nations. (Proverbs 18:15)*
5. *I AM a light in the darkness, illuminating the path to solutions for those in need. (Matthew 5:14)*
6. *I AM filled with divine insight, enabling me to see solutions where others see obstacles. (Colossians 2:2-3)*
7. *I AM an overcomer of challenges, and I rise above difficulties to find solutions. (Romans 8:37)*
8. *I AM a resourceful thinker, and I tap into God's wisdom to provide answers to the world's problems. (Proverbs 2:6)*
9. *I AM a problem solver in my workplace, bringing harmony and success to my team. (Psalm 133:1)*

10. I AM a channel of God's love and solutions, offering hope to those in despair. (1 Corinthians 13:2)

11. I AM a bridge builder, connecting people and resources to resolve issues. (Proverbs 27:17)

12. I AM a problem solver through prayer, seeking divine guidance in every circumstance. (Philippians 4:6-7)

13. I AM a peacemaker, facilitating reconciliation and unity among divided hearts. (Matthew 5:9)

14. I AM an advocate for justice, working to right the wrongs in society. (Micah 6:8)

15. I AM a problem solver through forgiveness, releasing the burden of past conflicts. (Ephesians 4:32)

16. I AM a visionary, seeing opportunities for change and transformation. (Isaiah 43:19)

17. I AM a steward of God's resources, using them wisely to address needs. (Luke 16:10)

18. I AM a leader who empowers others to be problem solvers and world-changers. (1 Timothy 4:12)

19. I AM a channel of compassion, extending help to those in crisis. (Galatians 6:2)

20. I AM a solution seeker, persistently pursuing answers to challenging problems. (Matthew 7:7)

21. I AM a voice for the voiceless, advocating for those who cannot speak for themselves. (Proverbs 31:8-9)

22. I AM a problem solver in my family, fostering understanding and unity. (Colossians 3:13)

23. I AM a servant leader, putting the needs of others before my own. (Mark 10:45)

24. *I AM a catalyst for change, inspiring others to take action for a better world. (2 Timothy 1:7)*
25. *I AM a warrior of faith, believing that nothing is impossible with God. (Mark 9:23)*
26. *I AM a problem solver through perseverance, never giving up on finding solutions. (James 1:12)*
27. *I AM a wise decision-maker, guided by the Holy Spirit in all my choices. (James 3:17)*
28. *I AM a messenger of hope, proclaiming God's promises of restoration and healing. (Jeremiah 29:11)*
29. *I AM a servant of all, following the example of Jesus in humility and love. (Mark 10:44)*
30. *I AM a collaborator, working with others to bring about positive change. (Ecclesiastes 4:9-10)*
31. *I AM a world-changer, making a lasting impact by being a solution to the world's needs. (Matthew 5:13-16)*

20. Prosperity and Financial Abundance

May these declarations and scriptures on **Prosperity and Finances** inspire and empower you to walk in financial abundance and God's blessings.

1. *I AM blessed with abundance because the Lord is my shepherd, and I shall not want. (Psalm 23:1)*
2. *I AM a giver, and as I give, it is given to me, pressed down, shaken together, and running over. (Luke 6:38)*
3. *I AM walking in the wisdom of God, making sound financial decisions that lead to prosperity. (Proverbs 3:13-16)*
4. *I AM declaring that the Lord delights in my prosperity and the prosperity of His servants. (Psalm 35:27)*
5. *I AM a faithful steward of what God has entrusted to me, and He multiplies my resources. (Matthew 25:21)*
6. *I AM declaring that God's plans for me are plans for prosperity and a future filled with hope. (Jeremiah 29:11)*
7. *I AM sowing seeds of generosity, and I reap a bountiful harvest in every area of my life. (2 Corinthians 9:6)*
8. *I AM blessed to be a blessing, and my generosity extends to those in need. (Proverbs 11:25)*
9. *I AM a receiver of God's abundance, for He supplies all my needs according to His riches in glory. (Philippians 4:19)*

10. I AM declaring that I AM the head and not the tail, above and not beneath. (Deuteronomy 28:13)

11. I AM trusting in the Lord with all my heart, knowing that He directs my financial paths. (Proverbs 3:5-6)

12. I AM walking in financial favor, for the Lord goes before me and makes a way. (Isaiah 45:2)

13. I AM declaring that I have an inheritance that is incorruptible, reserved in heaven for me. (1 Peter 1:4)

14. I AM a lender and not a borrower, for the Lord has made me the head and not the tail. (Deuteronomy 28:12)

15. I AM prospering in all I do, for the hand of the Lord is upon me for good. (Ezra 7:9)

16. I AM seeking first the kingdom of God, and all these things, including financial blessings, are added unto me. (Matthew 6:33)

17. I AM a wise planner, and my plans succeed as I commit them to the Lord. (Proverbs 16:3)

18. I AM declaring that I have an abundance of financial wisdom, knowledge, and understanding. (Proverbs 24:3-4)

19. I AM generous in my giving, and God blesses me abundantly in return. (Proverbs 22:9)

20. I AM declaring that I AM a partaker of God's divine nature, and prosperity is part of His nature. (2 Peter 1:4)

21. I AM declaring that the wealth of the wicked is laid up for the righteous. (Proverbs 13:22)

22. I AM a diligent worker, and my efforts are rewarded with financial increase. (Proverbs 10:4)

23. *I AM declaring that I AM blessed in the city and in the field, in all my comings and goings. (Deuteronomy 28:3)*

24. *I AM a cheerful giver, and my generosity opens the windows of heaven over my life. (Malachi 3:10)*

25. *I AM a receiver of divine ideas and strategies for financial success. (Deuteronomy 8:18)*

26. *I AM declaring that I have the power to create wealth, for it is God who gives me the ability. (Deuteronomy 8:18)*

27. *I AM walking in financial prosperity, and the blessings of the Lord make me rich. (Proverbs 10:22)*

28. *I AM declaring that I AM a wise steward of my resources, and God entrusts me with more. (Matthew 25:23)*

29. *I AM a person of integrity in my finances, and the favor of the Lord surrounds me like a shield. (Psalm 5:12)*

30. *I AM trusting in the Lord's provision, knowing that He is my source of true prosperity. (Psalm 37:3-5)*

31. *I AM declaring that I AM a child of the King, and the abundance of His kingdom flows into every area of my life. (Galatians 4:7)*

21. Protection

May these declarations and scriptures on **Protection** strengthen your faith and bring you comfort and assurance in God's loving care for your life.

1. *I AM safe and secure in the shadow of the Almighty, for I dwell in the secret place of the Most High. (Psalm 91:1)*
2. *I AM confident in God's protection, for He is my refuge and my fortress. (Psalm 91:2)*
3. *I AM shielded by the faithfulness of God; His truth is my shield and armor. (Psalm 91:4)*
4. *I AM unafraid of the dangers of the night or the arrows that fly by day, for God is my protector. (Psalm 91:5)*
5. *I AM under the wings of the Lord, and His faithfulness is my shield and buckler. (Psalm 91:4)*
6. *I AM declaring that no evil shall befall me, and no plague shall come near my dwelling. (Psalm 91:10)*
7. *I AM confident that God's angels encamp around me, guarding and protecting me in all my ways. (Psalm 91:11)*
8. *I AM declaring that I tread upon the lion and the cobra, and no harm shall come to me. (Psalm 91:13)*
9. *I AM walking in the divine promise of protection, for God has set His love upon me. (Psalm 91:14)*
10. *I AM trusting in the Lord with all my heart, knowing that He directs my paths away from danger. (Proverbs 3:5-6)*

11. *I AM covered by the blood of Jesus, and no weapon formed against me shall prosper. (Isaiah 54:17)*
12. *I AM standing firm in the armor of God, equipped with the shield of faith to extinguish every fiery dart. (Ephesians 6:16)*
13. *I AM a child of God, and He watches over me day and night, never slumbering nor sleeping. (Psalm 121:3-4)*
14. *I AM hidden in Christ, and no enemy can pluck me out of His hand. (John 10:28)*
15. *I AM declaring God's protection over my family and loved ones, for His hand is upon them as well. (Psalm 91:11)*
16. *I AM walking in wisdom, making wise decisions that keep me out of harm's way. (Proverbs 3:21-23)*
17. *I AM a conqueror through Christ, and no danger or threat can separate me from His love. (Romans 8:37-39)*
18. *I AM declaring that the Lord is my light and my salvation; whom shall I fear? (Psalm 27:1)*
19. *I AM resting in God's peace, knowing that His perfect love casts out all fear. (1 John 4:18)*
20. *I AM a vessel of God's protection, bringing His safety to those around me in times of need. (Matthew 10:8)*
21. *I AM declaring that the Lord is my strength and my shield, my fortress in times of trouble. (Psalm 18:2)*
22. *I AM standing strong in my faith, for the Lord is my rock and my fortress. (Psalm 31:3)*
23. *I AM trusting in the name of the Lord, which is a strong tower; I AM safe when I run to it. (Proverbs 18:10)*

24. *I AM declaring that the Lord rescues me from every trap and protects me from every disease. (Psalm 91:3)*
25. *I AM walking in God's favor and protection, for His eyes are upon the righteous. (Psalm 34:15)*
26. *I AM declaring that God's Word is a shield and buckler to my soul, guarding my heart and mind. (Psalm 91:4)*
27. *I AM dwelling in the peace of God, which guards my heart and mind through Christ Jesus. (Philippians 4:7)*
28. *I AM walking in the light of God's presence, and darkness has no power over me. (Psalm 27:1)*
29. *I AM declaring that the Lord is my shepherd, and I lack nothing; He leads me beside still waters. (Psalm 23:1-2)*
30. *I AM a victor over fear, for God has not given me a spirit of fear but of power, love, and a sound mind. (2 Timothy 1:7)*
31. *I AM declaring that I AM hidden in Christ, and His protection is my shield and fortress. (Colossians 3:3)*

22. Purpose and Fulfillment

May these declarations and scriptures inspire and empower you to **Discover and Fulfill your Purpose**, recognizing the unique role you play in God's plan.

1. *I AM created with purpose, and my life has meaning and significance. (Jeremiah 29:11)*
2. *I AM declaring that I AM fearfully and wonderfully made, designed for a unique purpose. (Psalm 139:14)*
3. *I AM a person of destiny, walking in the good works prepared for me by God. (Ephesians 2:10)*
4. *I AM confident in God's plan for my life, knowing that He directs my steps. (Proverbs 3:6)*
5. *I AM declaring that I AM a vessel of honor, set apart for God's use and glory. (2 Timothy 2:21)*
6. *I AM a person of vision, seeking the Lord's guidance to fulfill my God-given dreams. (Habakkuk 2:2)*
7. *I AM confident that God has equipped me with talents and abilities to fulfill my purpose. (Romans 12:6)*
8. *I AM declaring that I AM a person of impact, influencing others for God's kingdom. (Matthew 5:13-16)*
9. *I AM focused on God's will, aligning my desires with His perfect plan. (Romans 12:2)*
10. *I AM a person of perseverance, pressing forward toward the goal of fulfilling my purpose. (Philippians 3:14)*

11. I AM confident in my calling, walking worthy of the purpose to which I've been called. (Ephesians 4:1)
12. I AM declaring that I AM a vessel of honor, cleansed and prepared for noble purposes. (2 Timothy 2:21)
13. I AM a person of faith, trusting that God's purpose for my life will come to pass. (Isaiah 55:11)
14. I AM confident in God's timing, knowing that He makes everything beautiful in its time. (Ecclesiastes 3:11)
15. I AM a person of destiny, destined to make a difference in this world for God's glory. (Acts 13:36)
16. I AM declaring that I AM a servant of Christ, fulfilling His purpose with humility and love. (Galatians 1:10)
17. I AM aligned with God's kingdom purpose, seeking first His righteousness. (Matthew 6:33)
18. I AM confident that I AM a chosen vessel, called for a holy purpose. (2 Timothy 1:9)
19. I AM a person of courage, stepping out in faith to fulfill my calling. (Joshua 1:9)
20. I AM declaring that I AM an instrument of God's peace and healing in this world. (Isaiah 61:1)
21. I AM a person of vision, setting clear goals and pursuing them with determination. (Proverbs 29:18)
22. I AM confident in my identity as a child of God, knowing that my purpose is rooted in Him. (1 John 3:1)

23. *I AM a person of compassion, using my gifts to serve others and fulfill my purpose. (1 Peter 4:10)*
24. *I AM declaring that I AM a fruitful branch, bearing much fruit in my God-given purpose. (John 15:5)*
25. *I AM focused on eternal purposes, investing my life in what truly matters. (Colossians 3:2)*
26. *I AM a person of destiny, walking in the path that God has ordained for me. (Psalm 37:23)*
27. *I AM confident in God's provision, trusting that He supplies all I need to fulfill my purpose. (Philippians 4:19)*
28. *I AM declaring that I AM a vessel of honor, sanctified and prepared for God's use. (2 Timothy 2:21)*
29. *I AM a person of gratitude, thanking God for His guidance in fulfilling my purpose. (Psalm 16:7)*
30. *I AM empowered by the Holy Spirit to fulfill my God-given purpose. (Acts 1:8)*
31. *I AM declaring that I AM a person of impact, leaving a lasting legacy for the glory of God. (1 Corinthians 3:10)*

23. Renewing of Your Mind

May these declarations and scriptures empower you to continue **Renewing Your Mind with the Transforming Power of God's Word**, aligning your thoughts with His truth and purpose for your life.

1. *I AM committed to renewing my mind daily through God's Word. (Romans 12:2)*
2. *I AM declaring that I have the mind of Christ, filled with wisdom and understanding. (1 Corinthians 2:16)*
3. *I AM a person of discipline, taking every thought captive to obey Christ. (2 Corinthians 10:5)*
4. *I AM transformed by the renewing of my mind, walking in God's perfect will. (Romans 12:2)*
5. *I AM declaring that I have a sound mind, free from fear and anxiety. (2 Timothy 1:7)*
6. *I AM a believer in God's promises, and His Word renews my mind and strengthens my faith. (Romans 10:17)*
7. *I AM renewed in the spirit of my mind, putting on the new self created after the likeness of God. (Ephesians 4:23-24)*
8. *I AM a person of prayer, seeking God's guidance and wisdom to renew my mind. (James 1:5)*
9. *I AM declaring that I have a renewed mind that focuses on whatever is true, honorable, and just. (Philippians 4:8)*
10. *I AM a vessel of transformation, allowing God's Word to change my thought patterns. (Hebrews 4:12)*

11. *I AM committed to renewing my mind by meditating on God's Word day and night. (Psalm 1:2)*
12. *I AM a person of gratitude, thanking God for His Word that transforms my mind and heart. (Colossians 3:16)*
13. *I AM declaring that I have a renewed mind that seeks first the kingdom of God and His righteousness. (Matthew 6:33)*
14. *I AM a believer in the renewing power of forgiveness, releasing any bitterness from my mind. (Ephesians 4:32)*
15. *I AM renewed in hope, allowing God's Word to fill me with hope and joy. (Romans 15:13)*
16. *I AM a person of discernment, testing all things and holding fast to what is good. (1 Thessalonians 5:21)*
17. *I AM declaring that I have a renewed mind that is steadfast, immovable, and always abounding in the Lord's work. (1 Corinthians 15:58)*
18. *I AM a vessel of transformation, allowing the Holy Spirit to renew my mind daily. (Titus 3:5)*
19. *I AM a person of humility, recognizing my need for God's grace to renew my mind. (James 4:6)*
20. *I AM renewed in strength, waiting on the Lord and gaining new strength. (Isaiah 40:31)*
21. *I AM declaring that I have a renewed mind that is filled with the peace of Christ. (Philippians 4:7)*
22. *I AM a person of self-control, choosing to think on things that are pure and lovely. (Philippians 4:8)*

23. *I AM renewed in purpose, aligning my thoughts with God's calling and plan for my life. (Jeremiah 29:11)*
24. *I AM a believer in God's grace, knowing that His grace empowers me to renew my mind. (2 Corinthians 12:9)*
25. *I AM declaring that I have a renewed mind that rejoices in the Lord always. (Philippians 4:4)*
26. *I AM a person of faith, trusting that God's Word renews my mind and transforms my life. (Hebrews 11:1)*
27. *I AM renewed in love, reflecting God's love to others through my thoughts and actions. (1 John 4:7)*
28. *I AM a vessel of God's Word, allowing it to dwell in me richly and renew my mind. (Colossians 3:16)*
29. *I AM declaring that I have a renewed mind that seeks after righteousness and godliness. (1 Timothy 6:11)*
30. *I AM a person of courage, replacing negative thoughts with the truth of God's Word. (Joshua 1:9)*
31. *I AM committed to the ongoing renewal of my mind, becoming more like Christ day by day. (2 Corinthians 3:18)*

24. Righteousness of GOD

These declarations affirm your identity as the **Righteousness of GOD in Christ** and encourage you to live a life that reflects His righteousness and holiness.

1. *I AM the righteousness of God in Christ Jesus. (2 Corinthians 5:21)*
2. *I AM forgiven, and my sins are remembered no more. (Hebrews 8:12)*
3. *I AM justified by faith and have peace with God. (Romans 5:1)*
4. *I AM made righteous, and my heart is filled with God's love. (Romans 5:5)*
5. *I AM free from condemnation, for I AM in Christ Jesus. (Romans 8:1)*
6. *I AM clothed in the robe of righteousness provided by God. (Isaiah 61:10)*
7. *I AM declared holy and blameless in God's sight. (Ephesians 1:4)*
8. *I AM an heir of righteousness, an inheritance from God. (2 Peter 1:4)*
9. *I AM sanctified and set apart for God's purposes. (1 Corinthians 6:11)*
10. *I AM a vessel of God's righteousness, shining His light. (Matthew 5:16)*
11. *I AM dead to sin and alive to righteousness. (Romans 6:11)*
12. *I AM a doer of righteousness, walking in God's ways. (1 John 2:29)*
13. *I AM an instrument of righteousness, serving God's kingdom. (Romans 6:13)*
14. *I AM the salt of the earth, preserving God's righteousness. (Matthew 5:13)*

15. I AM blessed because my sins are forgiven and righteousness is imputed to me. (Romans 4:6-8)
16. I AM filled with the Holy Spirit, enabling me to live righteously. (Galatians 5:22-23)
17. I AM called to pursue righteousness and godliness. (1 Timothy 6:11)
18. I AM an ambassador of Christ, representing His righteousness. (2 Corinthians 5:20)
19. I AM an over-comer, conquering sin through the power of righteousness. (Romans 6:14)
20. I AM a partaker of the divine nature, reflecting God's righteousness. (2 Peter 1:4)
21. I AM declared righteous by faith, not by works. (Romans 3:28)
22. I AM empowered to live a holy and righteous life through Christ. (Philippians 4:13)
23. I AM an example of righteousness to those around me. (1 Timothy 4:12)
24. I AM led by the Spirit of God to walk in righteousness. (Romans 8:14)
25. I AM a recipient of God's grace and righteousness. (Romans 5:17)
26. I AM a citizen of the kingdom of God, characterized by righteousness. (Romans 14:17)
27. I AM a follower of Jesus, who fulfilled all righteousness. (Matthew 3:15)
28. I AM empowered to resist sin and live a righteous life. (1 Corinthians 10:13)
29. I AM a witness to God's righteousness through my transformed life. (Isaiah 51:7)
30. I AM an heir to the promise of eternal life through God's righteousness. (Titus 3:7)

31. I AM a child of God, born of His righteousness, and I live in His love. (1 John 3:1)

25. Spiritual Maturity and Growth

May these declarations and scriptures on **Spiritual Maturity and Growth** inspire and empower you on your journey of faith and transformation.

1. *I AM growing in spiritual maturity, leaving behind the elementary teachings and pressing on to deeper knowledge. (Hebrews 6:1)*
2. *I AM a disciple of Jesus, daily denying myself, taking up my cross, and following Him. (Luke 9:23)*
3. *I AM rooted and established in love, comprehending the vastness of Christ's love that surpasses knowledge. (Ephesians 3:17-19)*
4. *I AM a diligent student of the Word, rightly dividing it to grow in wisdom and understanding. (2 Timothy 2:15)*
5. *I AM an over-comer, for greater is He who is in me than he who is in the world. (1 John 4:4)*
6. *I AM declaring that I have the mind of Christ, and I discern spiritual truths through the Holy Spirit. (1 Corinthians 2:12-16)*
7. *I AM growing in faith, trusting God's promises and walking by faith, not by sight. (2 Corinthians 5:7)*
8. *I AM declaring that I AM a fruitful branch abiding in Christ, bearing much fruit for His glory. (John 15:5)*
9. *I AM a vessel of God's grace, serving others with the gifts He has given me for the edification of the body. (1 Peter 4:10)*

10. *I AM seeking first the kingdom of God and His righteousness, and all things are added to me. (Matthew 6:33)*

11. *I AM a person of prayer, seeking God's guidance and communing with Him daily. (Philippians 4:6-7)*

12. *I AM walking in the fruit of the Spirit: love, joy, peace, patience, kindness, goodness, faithfulness, gentleness, and self-control. (Galatians 5:22-23)*

13. *I AM declaring that I AM more than a conqueror through Christ who loves me. (Romans 8:37)*

14. *I AM a living sacrifice, presenting my body as a holy and acceptable offering to God. (Romans 12:1)*

15. *I AM a doer of the Word and not just a hearer, growing in spiritual maturity through obedience. (James 1:22)*

16. *I AM declaring that I AM renewed in the spirit of my mind, putting on the new self created in righteousness and holiness. (Ephesians 4:23-24)*

17. *I AM a builder of God's kingdom, working together with fellow believers to advance His purposes on earth. (1 Corinthians 3:9)*

18. *I AM growing in discernment, able to test and approve what is God's perfect and pleasing will. (Romans 12:2)*

19. *I AM declaring that I AM a light in the world, shining God's truth and love in dark places. (Matthew 5:14)*

20. *I AM a person of humility, recognizing that God opposes the proud but gives grace to the humble. (James 4:6)*

21. *I AM a seeker of wisdom, asking God for it without doubting and receiving it generously. (James 1:5)*
22. *I AM declaring that I AM equipped with the armor of God, standing firm against spiritual attacks. (Ephesians 6:10-18)*
23. *I AM a work in progress, confident that God who began a good work in me will carry it to completion. (Philippians 1:6)*
24. *I AM a follower of Christ, bearing my cross and enduring trials with patience and faith. (James 1:2-4)*
25. *I AM declaring that I AM not conformed to the patterns of this world but transformed by the renewing of my mind. (Romans 12:2)*
26. *I AM growing in love, for love is the greatest of all virtues and the fulfillment of the law. (Romans 13:10)*
27. *I AM a person of hope, anchored in the confident assurance of things not seen. (Hebrews 11:1)*
28. *I AM a partaker of God's divine nature, escaping the corruption of the world through knowledge of Him. (2 Peter 1:4)*
29. *I AM declaring that I AM strong in the Lord and in His mighty power, able to stand against the schemes of the devil. (Ephesians 6:10)*
30. *I AM a witness for Christ, sharing His gospel and making disciples of all nations. (Matthew 28:19-20)*
31. *I AM grateful for the spiritual growth I have experienced and excited for the continued journey of transformation in Christ. (Colossians 2:6-7)*

26. Spiritual Warfare
(Subduing the Forces of Darkness-Having the Enemy under Your Feet)

May these declarations and scriptures empower you to engage in **Spiritual Warfare**, knowing that through Christ, you have authority over the forces of darkness and the enemy is under your feet.

1. *I AM a warrior in Christ, clothed in the armor of God, and I stand firm against the schemes of the enemy. (Ephesians 6:11)*
2. *I AM declaring that I AM more than a conqueror through Him who loved me. (Romans 8:37)*
3. *I AM a person of faith, and my faith in Christ is my shield against the enemy's attacks. (Ephesians 6:16)*
4. *I AM filled with the power of the Holy Spirit, enabling me to resist the devil, and he flees from me. (James 4:7)*
5. *I AM declaring that no weapon formed against me shall prosper, for I AM protected by God's righteousness. (Isaiah 54:17)*
6. *I AM a vessel of God's truth, and His truth sets me free from the lies of the enemy. (John 8:32)*
7. *I AM confident in the authority of Christ's name, and I command every demonic force to bow before Him. (Philippians 2:10)*
8. *I AM declaring that I AM a child of the light, and darkness has no power over me. (Ephesians 5:8)*

9. *I AM a person of prayer, and my prayers are powerful and effective in spiritual warfare. (James 5:16)*
10. *I AM an overcomer by the blood of the Lamb and the word of my testimony. (Revelation 12:11)*
11. *I AM declaring that I AM strong in the Lord and in the strength of His might. (Ephesians 6:10)*
12. *I AM a person of discernment, recognizing the enemy's tactics and schemes. (2 Corinthians 2:11)*
13. *I AM equipped with the sword of the Spirit, which is the Word of God, to defeat the enemy's lies. (Ephesians 6:17)*
14. *I AM declaring that I have authority to bind and loose, and nothing shall stand against me. (Matthew 18:18)*
15. *I AM a person of humility, submitting to God and resisting the devil, knowing he will flee. (James 4:7)*
16. *I AM filled with the love of Christ, and His perfect love casts out all fear. (1 John 4:18)*
17. *I AM declaring that I have victory over all the powers of darkness through Christ. (Colossians 2:15)*
18. *I AM a person of worship, and my worship ushers in the presence of God, dispelling darkness. (Psalm 22:3)*
19. *I AM covered by the blood of Jesus, and no curse or evil shall prevail against me. (Revelation 12:11)*
20. *I AM declaring that I AM anointed to break every yoke and set the captives free. (Isaiah 10:27)*

21. I AM a person of courage, taking hold of God's promises and standing against the enemy's attacks. (Joshua 1:9)
22. I AM declaring that I AM seated with Christ in heavenly places, far above all principalities and powers. (Ephesians 2:6)
23. I AM a person of patience, persevering in prayer and spiritual warfare. (Ephesians 6:18)
24. I AM a vessel of God's peace, and His peace guards my heart and mind in Christ Jesus. (Philippians 4:7)
25. I AM declaring that I have the authority to cast out demons and heal the sick in Jesus' name. (Mark 16:17-18)
26. I AM a person of faithfulness, holding fast to God's truth and resisting the enemy's lies. (James 4:7)
27. I AM equipped with the whole armor of God, and I stand strong against the enemy's attacks. (Ephesians 6:13)
28. I AM declaring that I have victory over every stronghold, for Christ's power is made perfect in my weakness. (2 Corinthians 12:9)
29. I AM a person of gratitude, thanking God for the authority and victory He has given me in Christ. (1 Corinthians 15:57)
30. I AM an instrument of God's deliverance, setting the captives free and proclaiming liberty in Christ. (Isaiah 61:1)
31. I AM declaring that I AM more than a conqueror in all things through Christ who loves me. (Romans 8:37)

27. Stress Reduction and Relaxation

May these declarations and scriptures inspire and guide you in **Reducing Stress and Finding Relaxation** in God's peace and presence.

1. *I AM at peace in the midst of life's challenges, for the Lord is my refuge and strength. (Psalm 46:1)*
2. *I AM declaring that I AM calm and composed, casting all my anxieties on the Lord. (1 Peter 5:7)*
3. *I AM a person of rest, finding my rest in God's presence and His promises. (Matthew 11:28)*
4. *I AM relaxed in the knowledge that God is in control, and His plans for me are good. (Jeremiah 29:11)*
5. *I AM declaring that I AM a person of serenity, trusting in the peace that surpasses all understanding. (Philippians 4:7)*
6. *I AM centered in Christ, for in Him, I find rest for my soul. (Matthew 11:29)*
7. *I AM a person of patience, waiting on the Lord with a quiet heart. (Psalm 62:5)*
8. *I AM relaxed in God's timing, knowing that He makes everything beautiful in its time. (Ecclesiastes 3:11)*
9. *I AM declaring that I AM a person of gratitude, giving thanks in all circumstances. (1 Thessalonians 5:18)*
10. *I AM at ease, for I have the peace of Christ dwelling in me. (Colossians 3:15)*
11. *I AM a person of tranquility, dwelling in the shelter of the Most High. (Psalm 91:1)*

12. *I AM relaxed in God's provision, for He supplies all my needs. (Philippians 4:19)*

13. *I AM declaring that I AM a person of self-care, honoring my body as a temple of the Holy Spirit. (1 Corinthians 6:19-20)*

14. *I AM calm in the face of uncertainty, trusting that God holds my future. (Proverbs 3:5-6)*

15. *I AM a person of mindfulness, living in the present moment with gratitude. (Psalm 118:24)*

16. *I AM relaxed in my relationships, extending grace and forgiveness to others. (Colossians 3:13)*

17. *I AM declaring that I AM a person of joy, finding delight in the Lord's presence. (Psalm 16:11)*

18. *I AM at peace with my past, knowing that I AM a new creation in Christ. (2 Corinthians 5:17)*

19. *I AM a person of contentment, learning to be content in all circumstances. (Philippians 4:11)*

20. *I AM relaxed in my faith, for I know that God is my shepherd, and I lack nothing. (Psalm 23:1)*

21. *I AM declaring that I AM a person of Sabbath rest, honoring the principle of rest in my life. (Genesis 2:2-3)*

22. *I AM serene in God's love, for His love casts out all fear. (1 John 4:18)*

23. *I AM a person of simplicity, focusing on what truly matters in life. (Matthew 6:33)*

24. *I AM relaxed in God's care, knowing that He cares for me and sustains me. (1 Peter 5:7)*

25. *I AM at ease, for the Lord is my light and my salvation. (Psalm 27:1)*

26. *I AM declaring that I AM a person of peace, letting the peace of Christ rule in my heart. (Colossians 3:15)*
27. *I AM restful in my thoughts, taking every thought captive to the obedience of Christ. (2 Corinthians 10:5)*
28. *I AM a person of restorative rest, rejuvenating my body, mind, and spirit. (Psalm 23:2)*
29. *I AM relaxed in God's grace, for His grace is sufficient for me. (2 Corinthians 12:9)*
30. *I AM declaring that I AM a person of serenity, abiding in the presence of the Lord daily. (John 15:5)*
31. *I AM peaceful in my sleep, for the Lord gives His beloved sleep. (Psalm 127:2)*

28. Wisdom

May these declarations and scriptures on **Wisdom** inspire and empower you in your journey of faith and personal growth.

1. *I AM filled with the wisdom of Christ, for in Him are hidden all the treasures of wisdom and knowledge. (Colossians 2:3)*
2. *I AM a seeker of wisdom, and I ask God for wisdom without doubting, knowing that He gives it generously. (James 1:5)*
3. *I AM guided by the Spirit of Wisdom, and my steps are ordered by the Lord. (Proverbs 3:6)*
4. *I AM a doer of the word of God, and wisdom is continually increasing in my life. (James 1:22)*
5. *I AM wise in the ways of righteousness, and my path shines brighter every day. (Proverbs 4:18)*
6. *I AM slow to anger and rich in understanding, for wisdom brings peace to my heart. (Proverbs 14:29)*
7. *I AM blessed because I find wisdom and gain understanding from the fear of the Lord. (Proverbs 3:13)*
8. *I AM a person of discernment, and I rely on the Holy Spirit to reveal hidden truths to me. (1 Corinthians 2:10)*
9. *I AM surrounded by wise counsel, and I seek the advice of those who walk in God's wisdom. (Proverbs 13:20)*
10. *I AM a person of discretion, and I guard my words, knowing that a gentle tongue is a tree of life. (Proverbs 15:4)*

11. I AM a vessel of wisdom and understanding, and I use my knowledge to bring healing and restoration to others. (Proverbs 4:7)

12. I AM quick to listen, slow to speak, and slow to become angry, for the wisdom of God guides my interactions. (James 1:19)

13. I AM a source of wisdom and encouragement to others, helping them grow in their faith. (Colossians 3:16)

14. I AM a tree of life to those who embrace wisdom, and my words bring hope and joy. (Proverbs 15:4)

15. I AM a person of humility, recognizing that the fear of the Lord is the beginning of wisdom. (Proverbs 9:10)

16. I AM an example of wisdom and integrity in my work, always giving my best to honor God. (Colossians 3:23)

17. I AM a good steward of my resources, making wise financial decisions that honor God. (Proverbs 21:20)

18. I AM a peacemaker, using the wisdom of God to resolve conflicts and bring unity among others. (James 3:17)

19. I AM a person of gratitude, giving thanks to God for His wisdom and guidance in my life. (Colossians 3:15)

20. I AM a lifelong learner, continually seeking to grow in wisdom and knowledge. (Proverbs 18:15)

21. I AM filled with the spirit of wisdom and revelation, knowing God more deeply each day. (Ephesians 1:17)

22. I AM a person of faith, trusting in God's wisdom even when circumstances seem uncertain. (Proverbs 3:5-6)

23. I AM a wise parent, teaching my children the ways of the Lord and instilling godly wisdom in them. (Proverbs 22:6)

24. I AM a seeker of divine understanding, knowing that wisdom is more precious than silver or gold. (Proverbs 16:16)

25. I AM a person of patience, waiting on God's timing and trusting in His wisdom. (James 5:7)

26. I AM a person of peace, for the wisdom from above is first pure, then peaceable. (James 3:17)

27. I AM a witness of God's wisdom to the world, shining His light in dark places. (Matthew 5:16)

28. I AM a vessel of God's wisdom and love, sharing His truth with compassion and grace. (1 Corinthians 1:30)

29. I AM a person of character, for wisdom is demonstrated through righteous living. (James 3:13)

30. I AM a conqueror through God's wisdom, overcoming challenges and obstacles in His strength. (Romans 8:37)

31. I AM filled with the wisdom of God, and I trust that His plans for my life are good and filled with hope. (Jeremiah 29:11)

29. Worshipper of the Most High GOD

May these declarations and scriptures inspire you to be a **Dedicated Worshiper of the Most High God**, offering your heart, soul, and life in adoration and praise.

1. *I AM a worshiper of the Most High God, and I exalt His name in all I do. (Psalm 99:5)*
2. *I AM declaring that I AM created to worship God in spirit and in truth. (John 4:24)*
3. *I AM a person of reverence, acknowledging the holiness of God in my worship. (Psalm 96:9)*
4. *I AM filled with gratitude, thanking God for His goodness and mercy in my life. (Psalm 106:1)*
5. *I AM a worshiper who offers a sacrifice of praise, even in difficult times. (Hebrews 13:15)*
6. *I AM declaring that I AM a living sacrifice, presenting my life as an act of worship to God. (Romans 12:1)*
7. *I AM a person of humility, bowing before God in adoration and submission. (Philippians 2:10-11)*
8. *I AM a vessel of worship, allowing the praises of God to flow from my heart and lips. (Psalm 34:1)*
9. *I AM declaring that I AM awed by God's majesty and splendor, and I worship Him in awe. (Psalm 29:2)*
10. *I AM a person of surrender, yielding my will to God's perfect plan and purpose. (Matthew 26:39)*

11. *I AM a worshiper who seeks God's face, longing for intimacy with the Creator. (Psalm 27:8)*

12. *I AM declaring that I AM a joyful worshiper, rejoicing in the presence of the Lord. (Psalm 100:2)*

13. *I AM a person of praise, magnifying the Lord and lifting His name on high. (Psalm 34:3)*

14. *I AM a worshiper who sings a new song to the Lord, expressing His wonders and goodness. (Psalm 96:1)*

15. *I AM declaring that I AM a vessel of adoration, worshiping God for His infinite love. (1 John 4:19)*

16. *I AM a person of faith, trusting God's faithfulness in my worship. (Hebrews 10:23)*

17. *I AM a worshiper who glorifies God through my actions and attitudes. (1 Corinthians 10:31)*

18. *I AM declaring that I AM a thankful worshiper, counting my blessings and praising God. (Psalm 103:2)*

19. *I AM a person of love, worshiping God with all my heart, soul, and strength. (Matthew 22:37)*

20. *I AM a worshiper who seeks God's presence daily, hungering for His touch. (Psalm 42:1-2)*

21. *I AM declaring that I AM a grateful worshiper, acknowledging God's faithfulness in my life. (Psalm 89:1)*

22. *I AM a person of adoration, worshiping God for His infinite wisdom and knowledge. (Romans 11:33)*

23. *I AM a worshiper who offers my life as a living testimony to God's grace and goodness. (Psalm 66:16)*

24. I AM declaring that I AM a humble worshiper, recognizing my need for God's mercy. (Luke 18:13)
25. I AM a person of awe, standing in reverence before the greatness of God. (Psalm 33:8)
26. I AM a worshiper who seeks to align my thoughts and actions with God's will. (Romans 12:2)
27. I AM declaring that I AM a faithful worshiper, committed to worshiping God in all seasons. (Psalm 34:1)
28. I AM a person of surrender, offering my life as a living sacrifice in worship. (Romans 12:1)
29. I AM a worshiper who delights in the beauty of God's holiness. (Psalm 29:2)
30. I AM declaring that I AM a worshiper who magnifies the Lord and lifts His name on high. (Psalm 34:3)
31. I AM a person of worship, and my worship is a sweet fragrance to the Most High God. (Ephesians 5:2)

30. For Children-Declarations for Your Children to Confess/ Claim/ Prophecy over their lives

These declarations are designed to **empower and instill positive beliefs in children** based on God's Word.

1. *I AM Blessed (Numbers 6:24-26)*
2. *I AM Highly Favored (Luke 1:28)*
3. *I AM Fearfully and Wonderfully Made (Psalm 139:14)*
4. *I AM a Child of God (John 1:12)*
5. *I AM a Light in the World (Matthew 5:14)*
6. *I AM Strong and Courageous (Joshua 1:9)*
7. *I AM God's Workmanship (Ephesians 2:10)*
8. *I AM Loved with an Everlasting Love (Jeremiah 31:3)*
9. *I AM an Over-comer (Romans 8:37)*
10. *I AM the Salt of the Earth (Matthew 5:13)*
11. *I AM a Peacemaker (Matthew 5:9)*
12. *I AM a Blessing to Others (Genesis 12:2)*
13. *I AM a Disciple of Jesus (Matthew 28:19-20)*
14. *I AM a Child of the Light (Ephesians 5:8)*
15. *I AM Wise and Understanding (James 1:5)*
16. *I AM a Vessel of Honor (2 Timothy 2:21)*
17. *I AM God's Temple (1 Corinthians 6:19-20)*
18. *I AM a Fruitful Vine (Psalm 128:3)*
19. *I AM a Conqueror through Christ (Romans 8:37)*
20. *I AM a Servant of God (Mark 10:45)*
21. *I AM a Crown of Glory (Proverbs 4:9)*
22. *I AM God's Beloved (Colossians 3:12)*
23. *I AM a Source of Joy (Psalm 127:3)*

24. *I AM an Ambassador for Christ (2 Corinthians 5:20)*
25. *I AM Redeemed by the Blood of Jesus (Ephesians 1:7)*
26. *I AM a Peacemaker (Matthew 5:9)*
27. *I AM a Beacon of Hope (Romans 15:13)*
28. *I AM a Minister of Reconciliation (2 Corinthians 5:18)*
29. *I AM a Blessing to My Generation (Genesis 12:2)*
30. *I AM the Head and not the Tail (Deuteronomy 28:13)*
31. *I AM Destined for Greatness (Jeremiah 29:11)*

Conclusion

In the pages of this book, **'I AM Empowered:** ***Unleashing Divine Power with Positive Declarations'*** we have embarked on a transformative journey, exploring the profound significance of two simple words, "I AM." We have discovered that these words hold the key to unlocking the divine power that resides within us, the power of God's very presence and authority.

Throughout our exploration, we have learned that true power, the power that changes lives and circumstances, begins with a conscious awareness of the "I AM." Just as Jesus declared, "I AM He," and His adversaries were compelled to take a step back, we too can experience a shift in our lives when we harness the power of positive declarations.

The Power of Positive Declarations: Positive declarations are not mere words; they are gateways to transformation. They are the means by which we tap into the vast reservoir of God's Word and align ourselves with His divine will. Every declaration made in faith is a step closer to manifesting God's glory in our lives.

We have explored declarations on 30 various topics, from faith and healing to purpose and resilience. Each declaration serves as a reminder of the incredible potential we have within us, the potential to walk in alignment with our true identity as children of God.

Transforming Our Thinking and Speech: Throughout this journey, we have discovered that our thoughts and words are powerful. They shape our reality and impact our destinies. By choosing to declare positive statements in alignment with God's Word, we not only transform our thinking but also bring about transformation in our lives.

Living a Life of Purpose and Influence: As we conclude our exploration, let us remember that our journey does not end here. Instead, it is a beginning—a beginning of a life marked by purpose, influence, and fulfillment. By embracing the power of "I AM" and declaring it with intention and faith, we step into the extraordinary realm of God's divine presence and power.

May you take these positive declarations with you, applying them to your daily life, and witnessing the incredible change they bring. As you continue on your journey of faith, remember that the "I AM" within you is a source of endless strength, wisdom, and love.

With every declaration you make, you draw closer to your true potential, and you become a living testament to the power of God's name. May your life be a reflection of His glory, and may you experience the abundant life He has promised.

In conclusion, let us move forward with confidence, knowing that we serve a God who says, "I AM," and in Him, we find the power to declare, "I AM," with unwavering faith. May your life be a testament to the miraculous transformation that occurs when you embrace the power of positive declarations and align your identity with the "I AM" of the Almighty.

As you go forth, may your journey be marked by faith, purpose, and the continuous revelation of the extraordinary power of "I AM."

About the Author
'GERARD ASSEY'

Gerard Assey is a Graduate in Economics, a PGD in Management (HRD) and holds a Doctorate in Leadership. Gerard holds several International Qualifications in Sales, Debt Collection, Training & Teaching, and is a 'Fellow' of the prestigious 'Institute of Sales & Marketing Management'-UK, a Certified NLP Practitioner, a 'Certified Trainer', an 'Accredited Management Teacher-Behavioral Sciences', a 'Certified Competency Facilitator', a 'Certified Management Consultant'- (the International credentials of a professional management consultant, awarded in accordance with global standards of the ICMCI); and a Certification from the University of Michigan in 'Successful Negotiation: Essential Strategies and Skills'

He is also a Member of the 'National Association of Sales Professionals' backed with several years experience in varied industries, both in India and Overseas. He also holds an 'Etiquette Consultant' Certification from the USA (by Sue Fox, Author of Best Seller: 'Business Etiquette for Dummies'. She has trained some of the top celebrities' world over). He was also a recipient of a scholarship for extensive training in Japan on 'Corporate Management for India'.

Gerard Assey is 'Founder & Chief Corporate Trainer' of the Group: **'Citius, Altius, Fortius Unlimited'**- an organization that **celebrated 20 years of Glorious Service** in 2021, focusing on 3 Core Competencies:

People. Performance. Profit; in functional areas of Sales & Marketing, HR & Organizational Development, covering Recruitment, Training & Consultancy!

Having managed organizations with large Sales Forces in India & Overseas, his specialization cover extensive areas of Sales Training (All levels - Presentation, Negotiation, Key/ Strategic Accounts Management & Managerial Skills for all sectors), Bid Proposal/ Capture Planning/ Management Trainings, Retail Sales, Customer Service & Customer Retention Programs, Training for Prevention & Collection of Debt, Self & Personal Development Programs (Time Management, Teamwork & Team Building, Business Etiquette & Personal Grooming, Leadership & Managerial Skills, People Management Skills, Train-the-Trainer etc), including preparation of Custom-designed Business Manuals for Internal (HR, Induction, and Sales etc) & External use (Instruction, User Manuals).

Gerard has successfully conducted over 6000 Trainings & Workshops (as of Oct '23) all across India, Middle East, Africa, Europe & S.E. Asia. Besides public programs conducted regularly, both in India & Overseas, he has some of the top names as clients whom he services from Single Owners to large Public & Government undertakings, covering all sectors, for their in-house needs.

His website: www.CollectionSkills.com is the only one in this part of the world to be featured in the 'Collections & Credit Risk Magazine-USA' under 'Who's Who in Training' and ranks TOP, along with other websites listed below on most search engines.

Gerard is author of 83 books already (Oct 2023),

A Few of the Business related Books being:

1. Bite-sized Bits on Commonsense Management
2. Heart to Heart on Life's Principles'
3. How to become a Successful Manager
4. The Sales Professionals' Master Workbook of S.Y.S.T.E.M.S
5. The Professional Business Email Etiquette Handbook & Guide
6. The Professional Business Video-Conferencing Etiquette Handbook & Guide
7. Professional Presentation Skills
8. Exceptional Customer Service
9. Professional Tele-Marketing Skills
10. Professional Debt Collection Skills
11. The G.R.E.A.T. Sales & Service Workbook
12. Sales Training Advantage for Results (*The Ultimate Sales Training Manual to enable you stand out as a S.T.A.R.*)
13. CEO Daily Planner & Organizer
14. The Sales Professionals' Master Daily Planner
15. The Professional Debt Collector's Master Daily Planner
16. My Daily Planner & Organizer
17. MY EMERGENCY INFORMATION RECORD (Family Emergency & Peace of Mind Planner)
18. The Ultimate Therapist & Counselors Planner and Organizer
19. Building an Ethical Workplace
20. Managing Relationships at Work
21. Managing Business Meetings Effectively
22. Effective Delegation Skills
23. Goal Setting for Success
24. B2B Selling by Email
25. Professional Business Etiquette & Grooming
26. Dining Etiquette & Table Manners
27. Effective Networking Skills
28. Grooming, Etiquette & Manners for Teens, Young Adults & Future Leaders
29. Inter-Personal Skills

From the Ministry side, Gerard graduated in the very first batch of Charis Bible College-India & had for over 9 years served as a Part-time Faculty at Charis Bible College-Chennai (Andrew Wommack Ministries-Colorado, USA).

He is also a graduate of the Advanced Mentorship Program (AMP) and the Circle Of Ministerial Engagement (C.O.M.E.) of Prophet Jerome Fernando and a Spiritual Son of the Esteemed Prophet.

An accomplished author of several Secular & Christian Books, Gerard has been on the board of a few international organizations and boasts of being the SON of the MOST HIGH GOD: An ordinary guy following an extraordinary GOD!

Some of his most recent Christian Books being:
1. A Bouquet of Praises for My KING
2. Christian Jokes for the Serious Religious' Folks!
3. Jesus Healed You!
4. Praise24Ever! (also in Tamil version)
5. The 5G Network of GOD
6. Building Faith over F.E.A.R- FACE EVERYTHING AND RISE with JESUS
7. Hebrew and Greek Praise and Worship Words
8. Godly Mothers' and Grandmothers' Bible Story time for Kids!
9. Miracles of Jesus in Pictures
10. Raise your Praise all 365 Days
11. Thanking GOD with an Attitude of Gratitude
12. Meditating on the Attributes of GOD
13. Puppet Scripts
14. Alcohol Ruins, JESUS Reforms, Renews & Restores!
15. Habakkuk 2:2 Christian Daily Journal, Planner & Organizer
16. ABC of GOD's Word for Handwriting Practice
17. Daily Bible Verse Handwriting Practice (Building Godly Character & Faith through Cursive Handwriting Practice!)

18. Guiding Light: Fun & Faith-Building Bible Activities
for Children
19. *Rejecting Grasshopper Talk: From Grasshopper to
Giant-Killer-Defeating Giants Daily!*
20. *Teen Titans of Faith: Building Courage,
Determination & Christ-like-Esteem*
21. *I AM Empowered: Unleashing Divine Power with
Positive Declarations*

Besides regularly contributing to business & trade journals, including international ones such as the 'Creative Training Techniques' and the 'Sales News' of the U.S.A, He is also a member of several prestigious bodies & trade associations, having participated in many Conferences & Workshops in India & Overseas.

Prior to his last assignment of leading & managing a large MNC as head, Gerard had a 3-year stint in the Middle East as a Consultant with a leading British Consultancy Firm.

As the past 'Official Country Representative' for the International Business Award- 'THE STEVIES'-(the business world's own Oscar) for about 4 years- he ensured a few Indian companies that qualify for the same every year!

Gerard can be contacted at:
Email: training@Sales-Training.in,training@CollectionSkills.com
Websites:

       www.Sales-Training.in
       www.EtiquetteWorks.in
       www.CollectionSkills.com
       www.RetailSalesTraining.in
       www.SalesTrainingIndia.com
       www.ManualPreparation.com
       www.TrainingWithPuppets.com
       www.FirstContactAcademy.com
       www.SalesAndMarketingRecruiter.com

Our **TRAININGS & BOOKS** that can help your team

- ✓ **Sales Effectiveness**: Selling Skills for any Sector: Service/ Logistics/ FMCG Realty/ Insurance & Finance/ Media/ SPA's, Health Clubs & Salons/ Key Account Management, Effective Negotiation Skills/ Bid & Proposal Management Skills/ Retail Sales Training: Any Sector (Auto, Jewelry, Clothing, Luxury etc)
- ✓ **Customer Service Skills**-Complaints Handling & Customer Retention
- ✓ **Debt Prevention & Collection Skills**
- ✓ **Etiquette & Grooming**
- ✓ **Leadership & Managerial Skills**
- ✓ **Self & Personal Development Skills**: Presentation Skills/ Effective Communication Skills/Business Proposal Writing Skills/ Problem Solving & Decision Making Skills/ Empowering Secretaries-The perfect PA! (For Secretaries & PA's)/ Effective Time Management/ Teamwork & Teambuilding/ P.R.I.D.E- **P**ersonal **R**esponsibility **I**n **D**elivering Excellence